LOVE

HOPE

LIGHT

LOVE

HOPE

LIGHT

ANGELA MARTINI

Indigo River Publishing

Indigo River Publishing
3 West Garden Street, Suite 718
Pensacola, FL 32502
www.indigoriverpublishing.com

Cover Design: Nikkita Kent
Cover Photography: Giovanni Gastel
Interior Design: Robin Vuchnich
Editor: Regina Cornell, Jackson Haynes, and Earl Tillinghast

Ordering Information: Quantity sales: Special discounts are available on quantity purchases by corporations, associations, and others. For details, contact the publisher at the address above.

Orders by U.S. trade bookstores and wholesalers: Please contact the publisher at the address above.

Printed in the United States of America

Library of Congress Control Number: 2019950739

ISBN: 978-1-950906-20-8 (hardcover), 978-1-950906-21-5 (ebook)

First Edition

With Indigo River Publishing, you can always expect great books, strong voices, and meaningful messages. Most importantly, you'll always find ... words worth reading.

Contents

My Albania

My Albania—a place where poverty meant nothing to a little girl whose life was so thoroughly enriched by love. The city of Shkodër was my world—my safe, protective bubble where my dreams were born and I was awakened each morning from my sleepy flights of fancy to my mother's gentle voice, her kisses and massages. It's no exaggeration to say that I led a charmed life, with each and every one of my youthful wants and needs fulfilled. I enjoyed a universe brimming with activities, friends, playtime, and, most of all, my mother's presence. Her embrace was frequent and it was my most secure haven—my ultimate comfort zone.

The year was 1996, and I was nine and a half years old. I vaguely recall the rising tensions in my city and the occasional gunshots that would resonate through the streets. Such events were followed by a flurry of adult conversation: "They killed him! Did you hear? Oh, my God!" These words passed me like a feather in the wind. I lived in my own realm of joy and childhood indulgence. Young children don't understand the idea of impermanence—the reality that nothing lasts forever. It's as if an angel is standing over each child's shoulder, whispering: *Eternity is yours. Nothing will harm you.*

Then, one summer afternoon, as I was outside our apartment in the neighborhood of Perash during lunch hour (a time when I was supposed to be napping), the angel disappeared. I had begged my mother to let me go out and play. "Please? It's so nice outside and my friend is waiting. I'll be right back. I promise!"

Knowing she couldn't dissuade me—and since she perceived no harm in allowing me the pleasure of neighborhood play—my mother conceded. "Okay," she said. "But come right back."

My friend and I began our playtime, and it seemed we had the street to ourselves. No one else was in sight. The afternoons in Albania were basically a siesta. It was rare to see anyone on the streets. But that day, suddenly and out of nowhere, a man approached me as I played with my friend.

"You're such a cute girl. How are you today?" he began.

"I'm fine, and you?" I replied. I wondered why this strange man was addressing me, but I was very precocious and not at all shy.

So began a conversation that changed my life.

"What's your name?" the man asked.

"Angela Martini," I answered proudly, knowing the uniqueness of my surname in the region.

"Oh, don't you know? I'm a very good friend of your father," he said. "Where do you live?"

"Here, on the fifth floor," I said, gesturing toward my apartment. "But my father lives somewhere else. He's in Switzerland."

In 1990 my father had fled Albania in the first wave of refugees. He recognized the mounting danger amidst the political upheaval as our country bucked against corruption and repressive communist control. When Albanians were granted the right to travel abroad, my father was among the first citizens to flee. While most refugees were scaling embassy walls or pouring onto ships in evacuation efforts arranged with assistance from the United Nations, my father hopped on a plane and headed for Switzerland—a destination that led many to believe he was wealthy (which was far from the case). In actuality, my father had a great uncle in Zürich who could help him secure a visa—first for himself, and then for his family, ultimately arranging to have my mother and me join him there. Now, it was six years later and my parents had divorced. It was highly unlikely that my father knew this man.

"Come, let me buy you an ice cream," the man attempted to coax me.

"I don't want ice cream," I insisted. The treat meant little to me since my mother always indulged me at my first request.

"But I can give you the best ice cream," he said, grabbing my hand and pulling me away, leaving my friend to look on, bewildered.

As we walked, I spotted an old Mercedes with three men inside. Even from a distance, I could see the gold necklaces they wore. At that moment, I heard my mother's voice in my mind: *If anyone wants to take you away, from one place to another, or wants to give you something, never go along—never!*

Instinctively, I realized I was in grave danger and I knew I had to act quickly. Without taking a moment to think, I bit the man's hand, ran away, and screamed at the top of my lungs, "You want to kidnap me!"

The quiet streets of our neighborhood filled with people who heard my cries, and the man got into the car and left. My mother found me shaking on the sidewalk, white as a ghost, and she took me in her arms.

"Oh, my God! My child, my little girl!" My mother sobbed, as if she'd nearly lost her whole world. Enfolding me in her embrace, she led me back into the apartment. "We must be careful now, my Angela. These are very dangerous times, and we always have to look over our shoulders. Do you hear me?"

As she spoke, I placed my head on Mom's chest and felt her whole body quaking with emotional turmoil.

From then on, life was never the same. In the days that followed, neighbors reported seeing the same vehicle circling the block, searching. Perhaps the mistaken belief that my father was a wealthy man had put me at a particular risk, but in those days children were being sold into prostitution in Italy or kidnapped and killed, their vital organs sold on the black market—unbelievable, but true! At ten years old, I was already beginning to blossom into a young lady. I had long legs and long, dark, curly hair that framed my shoulders. My mother feared that these traits made me a particularly ripe target. Were all of us children at risk, or was it only me? It was impossible to be sure, and reported sightings of the suspicious Mercedes kept circling the neighborhood.

On the day that I was nearly kidnapped from my home and whisked away to unknown terrors, something clicked in my mother's mind. Our neighborhood wasn't safe for me anymore. Until this point, I'd been free to come and go as I pleased—even as a small child. While my mother, a teacher, was at work, I played on the streets with all the other children. We were free to roam. In fact, I was just six years old when I stumbled upon a neighborhood beauty contest and fearlessly hopped onto the stoop that served as the pageant stage. While my mother was in the classroom, I was out and about, being crowned Miss Perash! I was independent and safe and loved.

But the attempted kidnapping changed everything—or it was the first incident that seemed to trigger a cascade of changes. First, my mother moved me to my grandparents' apartment in another part of the city. She would visit me there every day, she promised—and with the exception of one occasion, she did. Each day, my mother went to work as a teacher and came to have dinner with me at her parents' place. I missed the pink walls of our Perash apartment, but as long as I had my mother around, I could adapt to anything.

Then, about a month later, my mother was forced to move out of our apartment, too. With Albania in the throes of its worst economic crisis in history, my mother fell prey to the era's prevalent

Ponzi schemes. With fraudulent promises of enormous returns, so many Albanians had been lured into selling their apartments and relinquishing their money to nefarious schemers—some promising 100 percent interest, though the only thing that seemed 100 percent guaranteed was the horrific financial impact on victims across the entire country.

As a result, my mother was forced to join me at my grandparents' apartment—an arrangement that I found perfectly warm and loving, but my mother understood that the situation was a byproduct of Albania's stewing conflicts. Scams were forcing hardworking people into poverty; medical care was substandard; educational opportunities were scarce. My mother could see the simple truth: in our country there was little chance for my future to hold anything more expansive than my grandparents' cramped quarters.

With these thoughts in mind, my mother spoke to my father, Eduard, and they arranged for me to live in Switzerland with him and my stepmother, Rita. My mother and father agreed that my future would be better served by leaving Albania. My paternal grandmother, Angelina, agreed. Since her mother-in-law had become a beloved best friend, my mother took Angelina's advice seriously. "There's no denying that Angela will have a better education and a brighter future in Switzerland," she told my mother as a plan for my departure began to take hold.

Of course, my mother fully intended to follow me as soon as she could secure a visa; she was as attached to me as I was to her. How she would accomplish the feat of getting herself a visa was anyone's guess, but the foremost consideration was my safety, which she would never compromise.

Despite practically living on top of each other, my mother managed to keep the plans for my departure a secret from the rest of us—even as she spent the whole summer preparing for it. As I anticipated returning to school in the fall, played under her careful watch, and skipped rope up and down the block, my mother obtained the requisite documents to send me abroad. This included a custody agreement, placing my care in my father's hands—a prospect that must've contributed to her sleepless nights as much as Albania's growing unrest. Silently and courageously, she prepared herself for our traumatic separation.

My mother had already helped my older half brother, Blerti, move to Greece to find greater economic opportunity, but this was different. Blerti was already twenty-two years old when he set out in search of a brighter future abroad. I was barely ten years old. I can only imagine what it was like for her to keep the Switzerland secret to herself, knowing, as she did, that each passing day was one of the last we'd ever spend together in Albania.

Though I remained unaware of the plan hatched on my behalf, even as a child, I understood that life had become vastly different once we moved in with Grandma Dava and Grandpa Muho, my mother's parents. I believe I must have sensed the increased tension in the air, though I can't recall anything specific about it. By contrast, I will never forget the day my mother sat me down in my grandmother's kitchen to inform me that I'd be moving to Switzerland without her.

Grandma's kitchen was smaller and darker than our own kitchen had been, and you could never be sure what kind of smells might be coming from the oven. I have always hated the smell of fish, and so my mother never cooked it in our old apartment. But here, at my grandparents' place, there were no such accommodations. That day the kitchen was simply warm and filled with comforting voices. It didn't seem significant when my mother set a plate of Albanian cookies between us on the plastic kitchen table; she was, after all, always willing to indulge me in sweets. I do, however, remember the nervous look on her face.

"You know," she began gently, "our country is dangerous and the future isn't very bright for you here."

I knew there were problems. We weren't the only ones to lose everything in a Ponzi scheme; so many of my mother's friends had been affected. But at my age, all of the bad news blurred together. The attempted abduction, my sudden exile from my beloved neighborhood, the loss of our apartment—all of this happened within just a month, and none of it struck me as particularly *bad* because there we were—my mother and I, together.

"The good news," my mother continued, "is that you have the chance to go to Switzerland to live with your father for a while."

Visiting my father was usually a weeklong holiday from school; I knew from my mother's tone that this trip was somehow different. Of course, I assumed she was coming with me—until she reached for my hand and said, "I promise I'll meet you there as soon as I can."

I had no reason to doubt her. When I first moved to my grandmother's apartment, my mother had promised to see me every day, and (with just one exception) she did.

And years earlier, before my parents divorced, my father and I had set out for Switzerland—just the two of us together. I was four years old at the time, and my father and I had flown ahead of my mother, hoping to secure refugee visas before her arrival. That attempt to flee Albania hadn't panned out, and we'd all ended up returning to Albania together. But my mother had promised to join us in our efforts in Switzerland, and she did. It had taken her about a month to get there, but, indeed, she came. I knew she loved me and she'd never lied to me.

While my mother soothed my apprehensions, her mother aggravated them. Grandma Dava was aghast when she heard the news: "What kind of mother gets rid of her own daughter?"

My aunts gathered at the apartment, eager to agree. "So selfish!" they insisted.

"You're all so ignorant!" my mother railed. "I'm not at all selfish. I'm acting in the best interests of my daughter. Of course I want her near me. If I were selfish, I wouldn't be making such a sacrifice. This decision isn't about me. It's about Angela's future."

Despite all of this nay-saying, my mother found validation with Grandma Angelina, for whom I'm named. Angelina played a role in Mom's life that was less like that of a mother-in-law than a best friend. Her wise judgment consistently served to center my mother and set her on course. "Everything will be fine," Angelina reassured my mother. "In fact, you'll have a much easier time getting a visa for yourself if you send Angela ahead of you to live with her father."

This sustained my mother's resolve. Of course the government would honor our mother-daughter bond. If I were already living in Switzerland, officials would facilitate the process of my mother obtaining a visa. Surely she could protect my future without sacrificing our bond.

And this thought helped her steel herself against her own family's overwhelming doubts. "What if you never see this child again?" Grandma Dava cried.

Just hearing these heated exchanges made me uncomfortable—fearful and uncertain about what was to come. But, as usual, my mother was my supreme comforter.

"Listen to me, my light," she said, holding me tightly. She always called me by such loving nicknames—my light, my heart, my sunshine, my north star. "Don't listen to them. You know I want only the best for you. You have no future here. And I promise you one thing for sure."

I looked into my mother's eyes and awaited that promise as if it were more valuable than gold.

"I promise that once you go to Switzerland, I'll follow you right away."

"Do you promise me?" I asked, even though I trusted her completely. She had all my life proven that her promise was her bond.

"I'll be right behind you," she said.

...

A few days later, I found myself on a bus, traveling to Tirana International Airport with my mother, Grandma Dava, and three of my aunts. Unlike my holiday visits to my father, the whole crew insisted on coming along to the airport. Throughout the ride my grandmother sat clutching my hand and struggling to choke back tears.

"Please stop!" my mother admonished. "Don't you see that you're upsetting Angela?"

My grandmother looked at me, as if trying to assess whether or not I was upset. As we headed toward the airport, I sat looking out the window, like any other ten-year-old girl watching the scenery pass by. It's true that Grandma Dava's concern was unsettling, but, much like my father, I wasn't one for showing my emotions. I'd be willing to wager that my face lacked any trace of sorrow or worry that my grandmother could detect; I'm sure she had no idea that she might be upsetting me. By contrast, no matter how stoic I seem, my mother has always, *always* been able to recognize my emotions even as I try my best to hide them.

I knew I would miss her terribly.

That day, I had mixed feelings about setting off for Switzerland, but fear seemed to elude me. *What is there to fear?* I asked myself. *I'm going to be with my father. Nothing terrible will happen to me.*

When I visited my father on holidays, he always took the whole week off of work. He'd take me shopping. He and my stepmother, Rita, would do their best to entertain me. I had no desire to leave my friends or my neighborhood, my doting and dear extended family, and certainly not my mother, but I did my best to keep calm: *Nothing terrible will happen. Nothing terrible will happen.*

At the airport check-in counter, a flight attendant took my hand to escort me to my gate. I paused to hug and kiss my mother, my aunts, my grandma. Everyone I loved most was right there, and I wasn't quite registering that I was really leaving them behind. My mother smiled and walked along beside me until we reached the security checkpoint. "See you soon, my light," she said cheerfully and laughing, letting me know, yet again, that there was nothing to fear. The flight attendant ushered me onward, and it was only after I passed through security that I turned to glance back at my mother and saw her weeping. Bawling. The floodgates had opened, and she could no longer restrain her tears.

Confused, I continued to board. *How strange! Why is she crying? What could be wrong? She'll be joining me in Switzerland in no time at all.*

As I boarded the plane, I tried to block out the image of my mother in tears. Back then, I was too young to understand the family history that made separations so very traumatic for my grandmother, but I had already accepted that she found my departure worth crying about. My mother's tears? I did my best not to think about them. Instead, I sat in my window seat as we rose above my Albania and I watched the cloud formations roll as they lulled me to sleep. How odd to look back on this now, understanding the extent to which innocence is bliss. Had I known back then the reality of what was ahead, I never would have been able to sleep.

II

New Best Friends

My father, Eduard, rarely showed his feelings and sel-
dom displayed paternal affection. This stood in striking
contrast to the emotionality expressed by my mother, her family,
and Albanian culture in general. There could be no greater contrast
than there was between the bawling maternal family I left in Tirana
and my father, who would be picking me up in Zürich and taking
me to the city of Basel.

My parents divorced when I was six years old. Their match was
hardly one made in heaven.

By the time my mother and father met, my mother had already
been married and divorced twice—both times to the same man,
Xhafer, the father of my half brother, Blerti.

When my mother and Xhafer remarried, Blerti was, of course,
thrilled to have his parents under the same roof again, but this
reconciliation was short-lived. When Xhafer proved himself to be
abusive the second time around, my mother gathered Blerti and their
belongings and she left—for good. Back then it was virtually unheard

of for a woman to relinquish housing in a divorce, but my mother was courageous, determined, and ahead of her time. There was no creature comfort, and certainly no *stuff*, more valuable than protecting her son and moving forward with her life.

It was also nearly impossible for a divorced mother and child to secure an apartment all to themselves. In those days, large families lived in cramped one-bedroom apartments, while, through the help of a university friend, my mother and Blerti had an entire unit to themselves. Of course this inspired a new crop of cruel neighbors to spread the rumor that landing in such an apartment clearly indicated that my mother had been sleeping with officials!

Though these comments offended her, my mother remained steadfast, determined to begin life anew with her son. Truth be told, the apartment was a mess—old and neglected, everything from the floors to the bathroom fixtures having fallen into a striking state of disrepair. In her typical style, my mother just took a deep breath and forged ahead. She was grateful for the apartment and for Blerti and for the teaching job she loved. She was a single working mother who felt upbeat about her life, a schoolteacher proving herself able to care independently for herself and her son.

Then, my father came along.

Still a developing country, Albania had been experiencing something of a building boom. Construction teams were working on the streets, houses, and bridges in her village of Shkodër and countrywide.

Back in Albania, my father had a career as an architect and engineer. He was impressively mature and industrious for his age. At just twenty-four years old, he had already risen to the heights of his vocation and was managing two hundred employees as the director of a company. It was common practice at the time for groups of workers traveling in and out of the city to transport teachers to and from their schools. One day, my father was managing the team that brought my mother to work. My mother was taken with Eduard's energy and his work ethic. He was about ten years younger than my mother, and the combination of his youth and his competence spoke to my mother's own independent spirit.

It's a true story: my parents met on a truck!

The short version of the story is that my father took an interest in my mother's background and offered to bring his crew to help her out in her new apartment. My mother was more than eager to accept his offer.

With nothing at stake between them but goodwill, my father and his team renovated the crumbling kitchen and the grimy bathroom; they refinished her beat-up floors. He put all of his workers on the job and transformed my mother's environment into a space that reflected the fresh start her life was taking.

Once the renovations were complete, my mother expressed her desire to retrieve some of the many things she'd left behind with Xhafer, and Eduard gathered his team to help. When the men entered the apartment, Xhafer couldn't contain his jealousy.

"Go ahead and take her things," Xhafer said. "But don't you dare touch anything of mine!"

"Your possessions are not the issue," my father replied, calmly and confidently taking control of the situation.

Nothing romantic had taken shape between them, but there was an undeniable attraction brewing between my parents. My father was energetic and kind, making sure my mother had the freshest milk and accompanying her on long walks through the neighborhood.

Finally, two months after helping her reclaim her possessions from Xhafer, my father appeared at Mom's apartment. "You're a lovely girl, and I absolutely adore you," he said, venturing to place his first kiss on her lips.

My mother was enchanted and felt entirely at ease. Soon, they became intimate. My father spent most evenings at her apartment, but kept the relationship secret from his parents for quite some time; not only was my mother ten years his senior but she also carried the stigma of divorce. This alone was enough to inspire relentless neighborhood gossip—not to mention that she already had a child.

My mother and father, however, were passionate and in love.

Grandma Angelina was remarkably open-minded even back then. When my father first entrusted her with the news of his romance with Mom, Angelina surprised him with her response: "You'd better be fair and respectful to her, Eduard. You must never disrespect a single mother."

"I really like her, Mother. She's a lovely person, and she has a good job."

"I'd like to meet her," Angelina replied, and she joyfully embraced my mother as soon as they were introduced. To my brother, Blerti, she said, "Come and give this old lady a hug!"

Fond of my mother from the beginning, Angelina would visit her and Blerti from time to time. She understood that my mother and her son were dating steadily. She hoped they would marry one day, though she knew enough to maintain the couple's secrecy.

Grandpa Muho, on the other hand, was furious when he learned of his daughter's new romance. "How could you fall for a younger man?" he bellowed. "He's only going to exploit you without ever committing to marriage!"

My mother hated to worry her beloved father, but she simply had to follow her heart. As soon as both families learned of the relationship, my parents began living together—out of wedlock, of course; my mother was hardly eager to dive into marriage number three.

And just like Xhafer before him, my father took a sudden 180-degree turn. He became intensely jealous and frequently accused my mother of infidelity—with a bus driver, a store clerk, a stranger in the neighborhood. It was as if my father would suddenly snap, his temper flaring and his rage escalating by the minute. My mother, however, managed to hold her ground. "Either you get out or I'll stand here screaming all night."

Grandma Angelina was already quick to stand by my mother's side. "I'm so sorry for my son's behavior," she said. "For the sake of your love, please find it in your heart to forgive him."

"I can't," said my mother. My father's behavior was simply intolerable, and she'd already endured the violent temper of her first husband.

My mother kept her word, and the two didn't see one another for a while. In response, my father began drinking. After a binge, he would spend hours standing under Mother's bedroom window; once he even broke down her apartment door. Sober, he'd stop my mother in the street, asking for forgiveness.

My mother's resolve was strong—and it only strengthened once she learned that my father had begun a relationship with her colleague's sister shortly after their breakup. Her coworker went on to detail much of what had gone on between my father and this new lover. My mother was unsure if these stories were true, but she was horrified either way, and she would not yield to my father's pleas for forgiveness.

"I love only you!" he declared with desperation when confronted.

Except, as it turned out, my father had become engaged to this other woman. "I was forced into it," he said.

"Forced?" my mother challenged. "What do you mean, 'forced'?"

He simply could not bring himself to answer. At first, my mother felt rejected, sad, and awful, but given all of the red flags surrounding the relationship—the infidelity and physical violence, not to mention their age gap—she decided it was best to move on.

But it wasn't long until my father announced that he'd broken his engagement; this time he was the one who'd been cheated on, and this fact seemed to chasten him. My mother decided to forgive him, believing he was sincere. Their relationship progressed, though it lacked a solid foundation, and my mother frequently found my father to be distant, detached, and tired. Still, she persisted in her attempts to make things work—and then, of course, she was pregnant.

Though I was officially unplanned, for months my mother had been dreaming of having a daughter. The dreams were so vivid, she knew in her gut that they'd soon become reality. Thus, my parents each reacted to news of this pregnancy in completely different ways. My father's reaction was almost a lack of reaction; he just stood there frozen in shock. My mother, on the other hand, was ecstatic. She knew from the get-go that she'd be having a daughter—she was absolutely sure of it! She was already excited by the idea that mothers and daughters tended to share a unique bond. *We'll be best friends*, she told herself.

Though my father was vehement as he accused my mother of infidelity, he was actually the one having affairs. Despite knowing this, my mother allowed Angelina to arrange for a wedding; she was determined not to have the baby alone.

My father had been transferred to the northern city of Pukë for work, and one day, my mother happened to find a picture of a beautiful young woman in his jacket pocket. It was inscribed, *To my love*, along with a phone number.

My mother called.

A sweet voice answered, identifying herself and her office.

"Hello, this is Eduard's wife. I found this number in his jacket and wanted to get in touch with him so that I can send the jacket to Pukë. The weather is getting colder," my mother said.

"Eduard's wife?" the young woman asked in disbelief.

"Yes," said my mother. "And I'm pregnant with his child."

When Eduard arrived home, he was silent about the phone call, but my mother had already communicated the details of the conversation to Angelina.

"I can assure you that my son will never return to Pukë," she said.

Given my father's emotional distance, it seems almost appropriate that he was literally at a distance on the day I was born. He was once again out of town working, but some animal instinct in him must have been triggered. He somehow knew that my mother was about to go into labor, and he rushed home that same day.

When he found the apartment empty, he then ran to his

mother's home, where she informed him that my mother had already given birth.

"Congratulations to the luckiest daddy in the world!" Grandma Angelina said, embracing him.

Dad could barely form words, but managed to ask, "Is it a boy or a girl?"

My father had already made it abundantly clear that he desperately wanted his child to be a boy.

"It's a girl!" Angelina reported with joy.

My father couldn't stop himself from crying out in despair. "Why? Why?"

In some respects, it was a blessing in disguise that men weren't allowed into maternity wards in Albania. My father was so devastated by the fact that I wasn't a boy, had he been let in, he might've caused a scene.

The next morning, he went to the women's hospital to visit Mom—though in Albania this meant standing on the sidewalk beneath her third-floor window, calling up to her from below. After a quick greeting to find out how she was doing, he asked, "Any chance you can come home with a boy instead?"

My mother was so smitten with me that my father's barbs struck her as more pitiable than painful. She quickly changed the subject. "Your daughter has your nose, as we predicted."

This must have piqued his curiosity. "Can you bring the baby to the window so I can see her?" he asked.

My mother carried me to the window, carefully presenting me for my father to see. Peering up at me, my father remarked, "Yes, you're right. She has my nose."

It's true that my father and I have always shared a striking resemblance, even when I was in my infancy.

I suppose I can somewhat understand why Dad nearly lost his mind over the fact that he had a girl to raise rather than a beloved boy. I realize now how very young and inexperienced he was when I was born.

I know he meant well, and I imagine that he would've found a certain comfort in the familiarity of his own gender. Even as a newborn, my femininity seemed to be more than he could handle, and he could surely mold a boy more comfortably with his strict, disciplinary ways than he imagined he could a fragile little girl.

Of course, he softened once I was brought home. When he returned from work, Dad would stare at me in awe, for thirty minutes at a time. "Stop staring at the baby like that," Grandma would say, shaking her son's shoulders. "Have you gone mad?"

"Is this really my child?" he'd ask in wonderment. "Is this my daughter? Look at her eyes and her cute little face."

"I did the same thing in the hospital when I breastfed her," said my mother. "The nurses would tease me for staring so intently I'd almost forget to feed the baby. 'You're so distracted,' they'd say. 'The little one is hungry and you're off in dreamland.'"

My parents named me after Angelina, who suggested the derivative "Angela." My mother was tremendously fond of her mother-in-law and ecstatic over her angelic, healthy child, so she was thrilled with this idea. In doting on me, my mother and Angelina bonded like best friends—and much of the time, my father joined in. It seemed that he lived for me, and we grew quite close when I was a little girl, even though his temper continued to flare. Still, it was clear that he wanted the best for his family.

In December 1990, Communism had begun to collapse and student demonstrations in the capital of Tirana had become frequent, having started earlier in other cities. In Shkodër, the first revolts broke out when a few hundred people demolished a statue of Joseph Stalin. Later in the year, regulations were relaxed, allowing for the freedom to travel abroad—opening up relationships with the outside world. With open borders, poor Albanians seized the opportunity to go overseas and begin a new life.

My father recognized that our country was being destroyed by the protests, strikes, and poverty, and so he was determined to apply for political asylum and rebuild our lives elsewhere. His uncle had escaped Albania years earlier and had already established himself as a doctor in Zürich—which meant we had a place to land outside of the refugee camps. My father and I would travel ahead and send for my mother once we secured her a visa.

I was only four years old when my father and I arrived at Markos's apartment. I adored both my father and his uncle. Neither of them knew a thing about caring for a little girl, but they doted on me, haplessly taking me out to buy clothes; awkwardly hovering around the tub, trying to figure out how to give me a bath; clumsily outfitting me in sneakers and dresses. In fact, there's a photo that captures the mayhem: there I am on the couch, decked out in nothing but sneakers and underwear.

Imagine two Albanian men and a baby, a sort of blockbuster comedy. They were trying so hard, but these men had absolutely no idea how to go about raising a child, not even Markos, who had a grown daughter of his own. I remember that we all bustled around town and laughed—how silly it all was!—but the comedy only lasted for about two weeks, at which point I began crying for my mother every night, wetting the bed.

"What do we do?" Markos asked his ex-wife. "We were having so much fun; what happened?"

"She needs her mother," his ex-wife said. "That's all it is. She must have her mother here."

This separation from my mother had such a dramatic impact on me that my father and his uncle had little choice but to do everything within their power to get my mother a visa in short order, which they did.

My mother and I had been apart for about a month, and the relief I felt upon being reunited with her was more powerful than I can describe. My mother and I have a particular bond, and just as we longed for each other then, I know we'll fervently long for each other for the rest of our lives.

III

No Place like Home

IN RETROSPECT, IT SEEMS LUDICROUS THAT ANYONE THOUGHT IT WOULD BE A GOOD IDEA TO SEPARATE ME FROM MY MOTHER WHEN I WAS JUST FOUR YEARS OLD. Perhaps the only thing that could be more naive was to think that I would have grown out of such longing by the age of ten—but there I was, on a plane alone, headed to Switzerland without my mother once again. *It'll just be a month,* I told myself. *It'll be just like last time: we'll probably only be apart for a month.*

I took comfort in the fact that Mom and I didn't stay in Switzerland for long on that first go-round. After she arrived, we briefly stayed at an asylum camp with others who had fled Albania. My mother, father, and I lived together in one room, sharing a bathroom down the hall with other refugees. I mostly remember sitting inside and watching cartoons. My mother couldn't stand the shared bathroom, and it seemed my parents' relationship had a tough time withstanding the close quarters—though, of course, the volatility of my parents' coexistence was hardly specific to our circumstances in Switzerland.

Fortunately, we were able to get out of the camp and into an apartment in Basel. Beloved wherever she goes, it's no great surprise to me that my mother was able to make profound human connections even under the difficult circumstances of seeking asylum. Natalie, the woman in charge at the camp, quickly came to love and admire my mother. Not only was Natalie well aware that our living conditions were far from ideal, she was also able to observe my father at his worst, wielding a temper and a relentless domination over my mother, bringing even more difficulty to our life in limbo.

Natalie suggested to my mother that taking language courses would help her adapt more quickly to her new environment, but my father wouldn't hear of it. He didn't want her straying from home for any reason. Instead, showing her characteristic wherewithal, my mother decided to teach herself. Natalie kindly brought my mother books and study guides.

Observing the discord that took place between my parents, Natalie tried to persuade my mother to leave my father. She promised to help my mom and informed her of government support, but my mother was convinced that my father would never let her go. Her only recourse was to rely on prayer and inner strength, hoping that someday she would find her own individual freedom.

As her domestic woes intensified, my mother began to consider Natalie's offer, but there was no way she'd have the Swiss authorities intervene, as her friend had suggested. More than anything else, my mother wanted to return to Albania—though such a return wouldn't be an easy feat. Beyond the logistics of travel and citizenship, it would be impossible to convince my father of such a plan. My father was perfectly content never to return to Albania again, but my mother and I deeply longed for our country. After some thought, my mother was inspired to try her hand at diplomacy.

"You know, Eduard," she began, appealing to her husband's sense of reason, "we're having such a difficult time here in Switzerland. I fear we're not even going to make it here as a family under these conditions. Wouldn't it be wiser for me to return to Albania with little Angela until you receive permission to remain here? Then we can return. Who knows? Surely it will be easier to get established here without a family to support."

The reality was that we were undocumented immigrants, and my father still didn't have a job. He was reluctant, but much to my mother's amazement, he agreed. "I fear you might be right," he admitted. "We're living under deplorable conditions, and of course I want our daughter to stay healthy and strong."

My mother nodded gratefully. She and I would return to Albania while my father searched for work. Then he could obtain the necessary papers and send for us.

...

The next day, with the help of his uncle, my father was able to obtain a visa for our return to Albania. My mother would have to receive permission from the authorities to leave the country. When this permission was granted, she learned that she'd have to be escorted out of the country by Swiss police—a prospect that she found horribly embarrassing. What would her family think if she arrived in Albania accompanied by law enforcement? Albania was still somewhat isolated from the world, and the people were unaccustomed to confronting foreigners—not to mention a foreign police force. My mother imagined a squad of officers flanking her as she stepped off the plane. With this concern in mind, she approached an officer. "Sir, do you mind if I ask whether we are going to be accompanied by your colleagues?"

My mother detected good-natured laughter from some of the officers in the room. "No, madam. We'll only be taking you as far as the airport in Zürich. We're not traveling with you to Albania," one of them reassured her.

"Thank you," my mother replied with a deep sense of relief.

The officer was amiable, but he quickly assumed a serious tone.

"Madam," he began, "if you don't mind, I'd like to ask you a question, and if you prefer not to answer, I won't ask again."

"Go ahead," my mother said.

"Are you sure you want to withdraw your asylum application, return to Albania, and take your daughter with you?" The look on his face was kind and he was undeniably respectful.

Mother was stunned, and her mental wheels started turning. She understood the officer's implication—that she should reconsider her decision. *Did I make the right choice?* she wondered. *What about Angela and her future?*

My safety and my future were always her greatest concerns, but when she thought about her husband, second-guessing herself came to an abrupt end.

She was always walking on eggshells around my father, afraid he'd decide she'd done something wrong and that he'd lash out at her. She realized how often she held her breath around him. Was there really a future for her and her daughter if they had to live in fear?

"Yes, Officer," she said emphatically. "I know what I am doing."

"Do you realize that once you sign the annulment of your asylum request, you're not allowed to enter Switzerland for five consecutive years?" the officer warned my mother.

Five years? But who wants to come back here anyway? my mother thought. *I've been through hell here.* "I realize that, Officer, but we need to go home."

With unflagging determination, my mother signed the required documents, and a veil of sadness came over my father's face. He looked genuinely repentant for his volatile behavior. My mother, too, felt a measure of remorse for all the love and history that had transpired between them, but the predominant thought in her mind was of flight, of escaping to freedom.

On the day that she and I departed, Dad continuously kissed my tiny hands, showering me with praise and assuring both of us of his undying love and commitment. "I'll do my best to make up for everything you have endured, Nexhi," he said at the airport, taking her in his arms. "I promise you that I'll find a decent job, earn a good living, get an apartment, and send for you. I promise."

As we boarded, tears filled Dad's eyes. My mother felt compassion for the man whose actions had driven us away, and parting was sorrowfully sweet, but on the flight home, my mother knew she'd made the right choice, almost immediately feeling whole and alive once again.

...

Throughout my life I've always found a certain glory in returning to Albania, and back then, with so many family members and friends still in the country, nowhere on earth felt more like home. "We made it," my mother said as our plane landed. "We're home!"

As we debarked the plane and navigated the Tirana airport, my mother carried the huge, beautiful doll I'd gotten in Switzerland. In Albania, most people still lived in poverty and children's toys were so plain and similar, produced in Albanian factories and distributed, it seemed, to all children as if they were standard issue. My doll from Switzerland, by contrast, was utterly remarkable—life-sized and strikingly lifelike. Such a splendid doll was something of a rarity even in Switzerland, and there certainly wasn't another toy in Albania that had been made with such care. It was no wonder that one customs official stopped my mother to puzzle over her paperwork. "It's noted that you're traveling with one child, not two," said the officer.

"Sir, I'm just carrying my daughter's doll. It's very lifelike, isn't it?" my mother explained with delight.

With a puzzled expression, the officer took a closer look. "My goodness," he said. "It looks so real!"

Such glorious objects had become fairly familiar to my mother and me, which, I suppose, gave us a slight worldliness, but my mother and I have always shared the same take-it-or-leave-it attitude about *things*; it's the people we love that matter above all.

Of course, my mother carried a certain guilt about our return to Albania. After all, there was no doubt that a Swiss future held greater opportunities for me, but there was also no denying the rallying power of family. We had barely made it through customs when Grandma Angelina appeared and seemed to fly into my mother's arms. Angelina had come to the airport to greet us, along with her other son, my father's brother, Marketin. This was home. We'd landed just moments ago and we were already in the arms of family.

IV

The Other Woman

BACK IN ALBANIA, MY MOTHER AND I WERE DOING FINE ON OUR
OWN. In fact, Grandma Angelina found it a relief that we'd returned
without my father, which gave her the chance to be around us without
the discord and volatility my dad's presence added to the equation.

Still, the plan remained in place: once my father secured a job and
a visa, he would send for us to join him. Once a week, my mother and
I spoke to my father by phone. This required a trip to the city's post
office, where we'd wait for hours on long lines along with so many other
Albanians calling to relatives overseas. "We'll all be together soon," my
father assured us. More than anything else, the post office made the
fact of our family's separation more palpable than it actually felt in our
day-to-day lives.

Having resumed her teaching position, my mother reveled in the
collegiality of her students. Now, with my father so far away, she could
dedicate herself to them without fear of reprisal for coming home late
and without suspicion that she'd been anywhere but the classroom.

I entered the first grade, and my brother, Blerti, left for Greece to live with Zana, my mother's sister. Blerti, too, was in pursuit of an adult life rich with the greater opportunities found abroad. My mother and I missed him terribly, but we knew he was safe and sound with Zana—and as soon my father could bring us to join him, we'd be leaving Albania as well. My father, however, wasn't making much progress on establishing himself in Switzerland.

Four months after our arrival in Albania, he informed us that he'd been denied political asylum for the second time. This time, he blamed Natalie, the woman who'd managed the refugee camp and had befriended my mother. "That woman never supported me," my father railed.

"How frustrating," my mother replied sympathetically. "I'm sorry to hear this."

Though she was able to utter these words convincingly on the phone, in truth, my mother found relief each time the reunion with her volatile husband was delayed. She wasn't eager to return to him in Switzerland, nor did she want him back in Albania with us. She knew that depression agitated his temper, and she could feel his mounting frustration and rage pulsing across the phone lines, joining us in the otherwise muted atmosphere of the post office.

"Call me tomorrow," my father beseeched in a sorrowful tone. "Where's your consolation? I need more support. Don't you see that this is a challenging situation for me?"

Of course, our situation in Albania was rife with its own challenges, but my mother and I were largely content just being together.

In the following weeks, my parents spoke frequently. My father's tone gradually took on a calmness, as if he'd begun to feel more at ease. It seemed he was starting to feel at home there, getting the lay of the land and making friends. Then one day, he made a stunning announcement.

"Nexhi," he explained to my mother enthusiastically, "I finally understand the trick to securing asylum. Some Albanian guys I met here explained that if I want to obtain my documents without any hassle, I should just go ahead and marry a Swiss citizen."

"What?" my mother was shocked. "How can you possibly marry another woman when you're already married to me?"

"No, no," he said. "It won't be a *real* marriage. I mean, it'll be official without being romantic."

My mother wished for privacy as she stood in the post office din as my father hesitated on the other end of the line.

"You and I can divorce, and I'll marry someone else," my father explained. "I'd pay her to marry me, and then we'd just go our separate ways. We'd never even live together."

My mother became extremely anxious, hoping to get off the phone and out into the fresh air. "Call me tomorrow," she said. "Why don't we discuss it then?"

My father heard the tension in her voice and did his best to reassure her of his devotion. "Don't you see? I'd be doing this for you and Angela. This is our only chance at a better life."

Over the course of a series of phone calls, my mother processed the information, trying to make sense of her own ambivalence.

"I beg you to believe me, Nexhi," my father pleaded. "There won't ever be anything between this woman and me. But such a marriage would be a lifesaver. It's the key to my becoming documented."

My father's reassurances only spoke to some of my mother's concerns.

"Listen, Eduard, I've thought it over, too," my mother said with a certain calmness and clarity in her voice. "I agree that this could be a viable solution, but please, can we keep this quiet? I don't want to go to court again."

In Albanian society, the stigma of divorce could be overwhelming—and this would be my mother's third, having already split twice from Blerti's father in Elizabeth Taylor–style, as she liked to say. She could feel the weight of carrying this new mark on her reputation.

"Don't worry about that, Nexhi," he said. "The whole process will be quick and painless. I'll send the money so you won't even have to travel to Switzerland, and the whole transaction can take place in a single day."

When my mother responded only with silence, my father marveled at the efficiency of the modern divorce, as if divorce itself presented possibilities as grand as leaving Albania behind. "Nowadays, money accomplishes everything," he said.

Before committing to anything, my mother sought Angelina's take on the idea. My grandmother seemed shaken but tried to maintain her composure. "Just think it over before you make a decision," she advised.

But my grandfather Muho, who never approved of the marriage, was delighted. "I never thought that fortune would smile upon you so quickly!" he said. "Divorce him, divorce him at once!"

My grandmother Dava also seemed pleased, and the surprisingly enthusiastic responses by her parents seemed to push my mother along, onto what felt like a wave, bringing a sudden momentum to her destiny.

A week later, when she signed her divorce papers, my mother felt a mixture of joy and sorrow. Of course, she was relieved to be free of my father's fluctuating moods and free to live her life on her own terms. Yet she was also haunted by the prospect of societal shaming. People were already starting to talk, gossiping that her husband had abandoned her—but he hadn't. Not really. The whole situation was just a means to an end, she reassured herself in the solitude of the evenings. All of this turmoil and limbo was just a means to an end.

As time passed, my father grew increasingly distant and their communication took on a rigidity. They spoke every week, but my father set a specific day and time, insisting that my mother call only on Thursdays at ten p.m. Sometimes it was difficult to believe that she still factored into his life in any meaningful way, but then she would receive a letter from my father, describing the difficult times he was enduring in Switzerland and promising to send for both of us one day.

My Two Dearest Loves,

I love you so much. Be strong, Nexhi. I promise I am working hard to provide for a better future for both of you. This is what keeps me persisting here. I miss you so! Please take care of my little angel, Angela. And please forgive me, Nexhi. I will write to you again soon.

Yours,

Eduard

Dear Eduard, my mother wrote in response. *We are safe and sound here in Albania, and you need not worry about us. We miss you, too.*

Her words resonated with truth. There was no denying that, despite everything, she still loved him. Longing for him one Monday as she came home from work, she decided she would break with protocol and call right away. *Why wait until Thursday?* she thought. *He's my husband; I can call whenever I wish.*

She turned her bicycle around and headed straight to the post office.

With the anticipation of hearing her beloved's voice, my mother dialed his number.

"Guten Tag, die Familie Martini!"[1] a female voice at the other end said in an upbeat tone.

My mother was shocked. Eduard had promised he wouldn't live with the woman he married. It was purely a marriage of convenience—strictly a formality. Yet here was a strange woman answering his phone and claiming to be family.

"Halo," my mother replied, slowly and deliberately, freezing in place.

"Wer sind Sie?"[2]

---

[1] *"Good day, the Martini family!"*

[2] *"Who are you?"*

"This is Nexhi," my mother stated without hesitation. "And who are you?"

"I am Rita," the woman said. "Eduard's wife."

My mother felt weak in the knees, struggling to speak. Regardless of the language barrier, it was almost impossible to find words. Their exchange slipped into a broken Italian, the only language the two women had in common.

"I'm calling because I must speak with Eduard about our daughter."

"I'm sorry," said Rita with confidence. "Eduard isn't at home now. I'll let him know you called as soon as he returns this evening."

"Thank you," my mother said, and hung up the phone.

Despite my mother's ambivalence about my father, this woman's answering the phone shattered something in Mom, forcing her all at once to face the reality that Eduard had moved on. This woman shared his home and answered his phone; this woman was building a new life with him.

Everything my mother had sacrificed in order to create a home and a family, to withstand a domineering spouse, to stay faithful to their marriage, and to forgive his infidelities and his tantrums—all of these efforts had been in vain. And the most upsetting part of it all was that my father had lied to her. *Why didn't he just tell me the truth about Rita? Why did he lie? Why did he play me like a fool?*

That night, my mother didn't breathe a word to anyone about her discovery. She spent the night alone, crying and thinking about my father. It was one thing to accept the reality of his marriage; it was another that he lied about it. She waited to confront them during their Thursday phone call.

"Hi, honey!" said my father.

"Don't 'honey' me," she replied. "Do you take me for a fool? Why did you lie to me?"

My mother was direct, appealing for a truthful answer, but my father—even caught red-handed—wasn't ready to give one.

"Nexhi, this is a misunderstanding. I don't live with Rita," he said. "All I want is for you and Angela to be here with me again."

It didn't matter what he said anymore. My mother knew better. She had heard the voice of the other woman, and she knew it was over for good.

"You can forget about me, Eduard. I'm moving on with my life. I'll pick up the pieces of my life and start again—just as you did."

"But you can't," said my father, lashing back. "You're over forty, and you're thinking of remarrying?"

Beyond her age, my mother had multiple divorces and two children under her belt. All of these things worked against her in Albanian culture, but she was determined to achieve self-reliance and satisfaction. It was quite remarkable for a woman in this world to forge ahead with her eye trained only on our future.

My mother found a job in the city, and we settled into a comfortable routine. Grandma Angelina was always there to support her daughter-in-law and to help keep the breakup a secret in order to avoid the backlash of neighborhood gossip.

Of course, I knew nothing of what my mother endured at this time—until the night I found her crying in her room. She was holding a letter from my father, who continued to write to her, promising to send for us; promising he'd make a life for all of us in Switzerland.

"What's wrong?" I asked as I approached. "Why are you crying?"

Mother sat silently for what seemed like a long time, until she extended her hand, reaching for me. "Come here, darling."

I walked toward her without saying a word, wondering what she had to tell me.

"Your father and I had some difficulties, and we broke up," she said. "Which means he won't be coming back."

I was a strong-minded child, in tune with my surroundings. I didn't understand the details of what was happening, but I felt the tension that had always pervaded my young life. Therefore, I spoke honestly and from the heart. "So what?" I asked. "What difference does it make? We're fine like this—with just the two of us."

I loved my father and I knew he loved me, but I could live without him in my everyday life; it was my mother's presence that made me feel complete.

V

Right Behind You

Prior to my attempted abduction, I began to be haunted by a recurring nightmare. The dream took place in our Perash apartment, the one I had to leave after the incident occurred. In the dream, I opened the door to our fifth-floor balcony and jumped out. As I anticipated the fall, I began to wave my arms up and down in a motion somewhere between swimming and flying. Just before I landed on the pavement, I'd jolt awake in a horrified state, crying hysterically. I had this dream yet again on the plane to Switzerland.

At the time, I was sure the dream suggested a certain doom, though in retrospect I wonder if it was more likely an indication of my own awareness that my life had suddenly come to seem like a series of narrow escapes. Maybe a certain predisposition to survival and luck has been etched in my ancestral DNA.

My mother's father—my grandpa Muho—certainly carries the gene. Muho Ibrahimi ("Zani") was born a Muslim in Shkodër in November 1925. He grew up to fight in the Second World War, alongside future politician Kadri Hazbiu, in the Albanian National

Liberation Movement, an anti-fascist resistance organization.

In 1943, at the age of eighteen, Muho was captured along with his best friend, Ramadan. Together they were taken first to a Nazi prison camp in Pristine, Kosovo, and then transferred three months later to Austria's Mauthausen, one of the largest and toughest camps in all of German-occupied Europe.

United not just by their convictions and the beliefs they'd been fighting for, the boys were both far from home, and they shared a language, a culture, and a crucial familiarity. The company of one another brought, at least for a time, some small sense of strength to their powerlessness, some small sense of hope to the bleak truth of the camp.

One day all of the prisoners were forced from the barracks to stand in the middle of the dusty road that cut through the camp. They were instructed to arrange themselves side by side, shoulder to shoulder, their weakened bodies forming a line that spanned from one end of the camp toward the other. Muho stood with one shoulder pressed against his friend's and the other pressed against a prisoner from the same barrack.

It was never good news when the prisoners were rallied out into the road. The Nazi officers had devised a variety of barbaric games, all of which resulted in horrific displays of public execution. Sometimes the Nazis selected a prisoner or two and called on them to stand before the rest of the prison's population. The selected prisoners always knew what was coming, and so they stood sweating and soiling themselves, faces contorted in terror as they waited, helpless to stop the bullets from being fired and helpless to hasten the firing and put an end to the torture.

On this particular occasion, the Nazi officers had concocted a new and particularly brutal plan: With the entire prison population lined up before them, the officers arranged themselves at the opposite edge of the road, facing the prisoners with weapons drawn. Every third prisoner would be shot, they explained. They'd start at one end of the line and count—*Eins. Zwei. Drei!*—then an officer would aim his weapon and kill whichever prisoner fell into its site at the count of three. Then they'd repeat the process all the way down the row, reducing the prison population by a third in just minutes.

Grandpa Muho knew that prisoners died at Mauthausen every day, their frail bodies collapsing under the burden of rocks they were forced to quarry and carry, or they were gassed, injected, or otherwise exterminated. *Is any particular means of death better or worse than any other?* Muho wondered. Second by second, as he choked back his fear, it was becoming increasingly clear to Muho that the manner of one's death mattered far less than one's manner of living. He stared ahead at the poised weapons and waited, helpless.

The day was hot and the road was dusty. Muho could hear a crow caw in the distance. Other than that it was silent. Muho thought of the warm milk-and-bread breakfasts he'd loved as a child; he thought of the poems he'd long ago memorized in school. He looked down at his feet and the reddish-brown ants marching methodically around the hill they'd built. All around him he could hear his fellow prisoners begin to cry and pray.

Eins.
Zwei.
Drei!

The first shot cracked the air. Muho had no idea who'd taken the bullet, but he couldn't even turn his head to look around before the count began again.

Eins.
Zwei.
Drei!

Again, the explosion and its reverberation shook the world. Muho's eyes were closed. It was as if his senses had shut down; even with his eyes open he couldn't seem to focus.

Eins.
Zwei.
Drei!

This time Muho heard a body collapse, the sack of it falling to the ground followed by the gasps of the prisoners to his left.

Only two prisoners stood between Muho and the man who'd just fallen. Muho was next; he was sure. He closed his eyes and awaited his execution.

Eins.
Zwei.
—

There was a sudden scream, and Muho opened his eyes just in time to see the commotion. Another prisoner had panicked and started running, so the Nazis shot him in the back. Then a solitary Nazi officer stepped forward to shoot the dying man yet again, this time in the head.

Eins.
Zwei.
Drei!

The officers resumed their count, but Muho was now the second man in the row instead of the third; the bullet that had—just seconds ago!—been destined for him was now aimed at dear Ramadan.

The sound of the gunshot broke across the sky, and Muho could feel its impact in his own chest as his friend was struck. He felt a pelting of blood on his face—a spattering immediately following the weapon's report. *Had he been hit as well? Was the blood his own?*

The thought had barely registered in his mind when Muho felt the dead weight of his friend fall heavily against his shoulder. He opened his eyes in time to see the last bit of motion as Ramadan slumped and fell to the ground, the depleted weight of him landing on Muho's feet.

Eins.
Zwei.
Drei!

The counts continued, each punctuated by another bullet exploding, and Muho could picture the series of bodies collapsing along the line, slumping to the ground just as Ramadan had. The dirt road at Muho's feet grew dark as it absorbed the blood of his friend who had come to seem like a brother.

Muho was devastated. He would go on to mourn this friend for the rest of his life, making a habit out of swearing on Ramadan's name in a pledge never to forget him. Everyone who knew and loved Muho understood the impact this barbaric incident had on him. There was no one who better understood the extent to which life is fleeting and just how utterly random survival can be.

Of course, putting me on a Zürich-bound plane might have enabled me to narrowly escape abduction by that particular man or dodge an errant bullet ricocheting from one of the riots that were becoming ever more frequent on Albania's streets—and neither of these "narrow escapes" compares to Muho's experience in the camps—but I've grown to question the value of organizing one's life around the avoidance of the bad at the expense of making sure to keep yourself orbiting around everything you love most.

Again, the dream had my arms waving. Was I swimming or flying? Flying or swimming? But just before I landed with a smack on the pavement, I woke—this time startled by the sound of the flight attendant's voice on the overhead speaker. "Willkommen in Zürich!"

I knew this meant welcome to Zürich, but the words served to remind me that they were basically the only German I knew. I heard a faint cry rising from my throat. I was awake and safe, but suddenly on another planet, as if I really had just dropped from the sky. My mother wasn't there to rescue me. I was alone and completely unaware that my mother and the life I once knew had suddenly become so far out of reach that sometimes I'd wonder if they were ever there at all.

...

My father and Rita were waiting at the airport to receive me. I don't think I knew that Rita's voice on my father's phone was the very thing that sparked my parents' divorce, but I did know Rita. I'd met her several times over the previous few years when visiting my father over school holidays. She'd always been nice enough, though never particularly warm. She didn't have children of her own, and she always seemed content not to have them.

They both hugged me warmly in the airport, but I knew things were different as soon as we got in the car. "Listen," my father said. "You'd better delete Albania from your brain. You're a grown-up and you need to focus on your life here."

I don't remember what prompted this comment; maybe I'd mentioned missing my mother. I'm sure my father must've meant well, but I was not at all a grown-up; I was ten years old, longing for my mother and for my country, and this command to forget everything I knew and loved was less instructive than it was terrifying. I didn't know what to say in response, and so I was quiet on the way back to their apartment.

Their apartment building was nothing special by Swiss standards, though it was much nicer than the standard communist-bloc buildings across Albania. Of course, I didn't care about that. I still longed for the fifth-floor walk-up with the pink-painted walls that I'd been moved from immediately after the kidnapping attempt.

There was a bed for me in the corner of the room my dad and Rita used as a home gym and office. There was a huge closet, but it was completely full of their things, so they gave me a box I was told to use as a closet.

When I'd visited over holidays my father would take the week off from work; he'd drop everything to whisk me around town. One time, Grandma Angelina came from Albania with me. Rita would join us, of course, but looking back on it, I realize I'd probably never spent any time with her alone.

This time, however, my father wasn't taking time off to buffer the shock of my arrival. Instead, he gave Rita some money to take me shopping for new clothes. She sat with me in the dressing room, just as my mother would have done, but as I tried on sweaters and dresses and looked to her for approval, there was nothing validating in her gaze.

I'd been winning a number of neighborhood beauty pageants back in Albania, and I'd received a fair amount of attention from neighbors and friends, who doted on my long hair and long limbs. I'd never taken any of this particularly seriously; I was just a child and these pageants were just a game to me. I'd stumbled upon the first one at the age of six when my mother was at work. I'd run home to find myself an outfit from her closet, dressing myself in her underwear to walk across the stage. I was a ham: precocious and confident. The way Rita looked at me made me wish, for the first time in my life, that I could be invisible.

It was clear almost immediately that Rita's attitude toward me had somehow changed or that she was willing to display previously hidden aspects of it. The day I arrived, I'd asked my father if he still had the paper and paints I'd played with last time. "Of course," he said, and when he brought them to me, I began to paint right there on my little bed. I knew right away from Rita's look that I'd done something wrong. She glared at my father, a scolding look he ignored, but that was the last time I can remember in that household when his impulses drove him to take my side. After that, it seemed he'd gone blunt when it came to noticing the strange dynamics between Rita and me.

Both she and my father left early in the morning for work, but Rita returned in the afternoon and was home with me alone for several hours each day. She imposed many rules—what I was and wasn't allowed to eat; what I was and wasn't allowed to do in the apartment, which I wasn't allowed to leave, other than spending an hour or two out in the world with my father on weekends.

Because I was not yet documented, I couldn't go to school. And for the same reason, I hardly ever got to leave the house. What did they think might happen if I went outside and revealed to someone—anyone—that I'd just arrived from Albania and didn't have my papers yet? Did they really think I'd be deported even though my dad had become a Swiss citizen? This alone entitled me to live with him.

Back in Albania, the streets were always filled with children. The sound of laughter carried across the air, and you could find a group of kids anywhere you looked; you could just run outside and join the play—just look out your window and you'd be sure to spot a friend.

When I looked out the apartment windows, there were only two things I could see: either empty streets without a pulse or the gray concrete of the building next door. "Are all the children dead here?" I asked my father early on.

The culture was entirely unfamiliar to me, and it would stay that way for quite some time. I spoke no German; I had no friends, nowhere to go, and nothing to do.

The only thing worse than all those hours alone were the hours each afternoon when Rita returned from work and it was just the two of us in that apartment together. I suppose her inconsistency was the most uncomfortable thing. Sometimes everything seemed just fine—she was generally on her best behavior when my father was around—and sometimes, unpredictably, it seemed like my presence made her mean. There was never a singular, major affront; rather, the discomfort was due to the steady current of smaller indignities. I was not allowed to open the refrigerator unless she was home. She would heat up a Swiss breakfast for my father and insist that I ate mine cold. If I were reading on my bed, she might tell me she needed the office and kick me out of the room. The cumulative effect, of course, was that she kept me on edge—all day, every day—and I was only ten years old.

I'd moved from my mother and my beloved home to this strange apartment with my strange stepmother with nothing to do each and every day. Each night, I'd lie in bed wondering what I'd done that was so awful God had to punish me this way. Then my father would wake at five a.m. to lift his weights and do his exercises, and I'd begin yet another dreadful day to the sounds of his footwork and labored breathing.

Imagine being uprooted from your home, your mother, your friends, your family, your language. Imagine being ten years old in an apartment alone all day, with nowhere to go—no school, no teachers, no friends, no familiar foods, no cell phone in your pocket, nothing but hope and longing getting you through each day.

"I'll be right behind you," my mother had said. These were the first words to pop into my head every morning and the last words I thought about as I drifted off each night.

VI

Caught in the Crossfire

BACK IN ALBANIA, MY MOTHER MANAGED TO REMAIN STRONG AND STOIC EACH DAY AT WORK, FINDING COMFORT IN THE CLASSROOM. She was a natural and brilliant teacher, and her commitment to the students helped distract her from my absence, but upon her return each afternoon to my grandparents' apartment, her emotions swelled and the floodgates opened. Without a husband or partner and with both of her children living abroad, she became despondent. Were it not for her job, she wouldn't have had an outlet at all. Teaching was her salvation, but sometimes, even on her most enjoyable days, she couldn't wait to get home, let down her guard, and cry.

Conditions were declining in Albania. One afternoon, when my mother and Grandmother Dava were on their way to the post office to call me in Switzerland, they were caught in the middle of an outbreak of gunfire—first hearing the gunshots crack the air and then actually seeing the bullets whirring past. They took shelter as best they could alongside a building, pressing themselves against the structure and hoping they wouldn't end up casualties of gun-toting civilians. Fortunately, the gunfire ceased, and after a few minutes they emerged from hiding and got back on their way, resuming their route as if nothing out of the ordinary had happened.

Of course, the gunfire resounded for my mother, validating the decision to send me away and serving as a reminder of how imperative it was for her to escape Albania as well.

When she arrived at the post office, my mother stood in the phone booth for a few minutes to catch her breath and collect herself, never expecting that her call would be met with a different sort of attack.

"Hello, Eduard," she said, pleasant as always. "May I speak to Angela, please?"

"Absolutely," said my father. "But there's something I want to discuss with you first."

My mother says that her heart sank to her stomach in this moment; there was something in his tone that made it clear that trouble was afoot.

"Nexhi," my father said forcefully, "if you really want to secure documents for Angela to live here in Switzerland, then you really only have one choice."

My father proceeded to explain that the daughter of a Swiss woman would be guaranteed documentation. All my mother had to do was to authorize Rita to adopt me.

This wasn't true, of course. My father's Swiss citizenship was enough to garner my documentation, and once I was documented, it would be much easier for my mother to join me. The government respected the bond between mother and daughter. And this was the problem. Though Rita had no real interest in being my mother, she certainly didn't want my mother around, and so this plan was designed not to facilitate my immigration status but to sabotage my mom's. I am not sure why, exactly, my father decided to play along, but he did.

"All you have to do," said my father, "is sign the papers authorizing Rita to adopt Angela."

Nausea overtook my mother, but she rallied herself. She stood straight in the phone booth and managed to pull herself together. This characteristic has defined her throughout most of her life. "No, Eduard," she said. "I can't and I won't allow that to happen."

When the call ended, my mother's head was reeling. *This is madness. My daughter adopted by a stranger? Never!*

Once she had time to process my father's request, my mother called back the following day. Rita answered the phone. Once again, the conversation took place in halting Italian. "Eduard isn't home, and Angela isn't here right now either," Rita said, as I stood nearby, listening to the conversation in horror and disbelief.

This was in January of 1997. I was a month into my sustained culture shock, uprooted from the home I loved and finding no comfort anywhere in this new world. A chill wind suddenly surrounded my young life. *Everything* had changed. I felt the coldness of the people around me and the coldness of the house itself. Rita made it clear that I was never to open the refrigerator without asking her first, and so I was surviving on the room-temperature yogurts stored on the shelf. Forget about my fantasies of beloved Albanian comfort foods; unless my father was home, I hardly had a hot meal. Even the morning sun seemed dimmer than it used to be in my Albania. I felt lost without my mother's touch and tender words to wake me from my dreams, and I felt punished with all the ways Rita kept me on edge.

Living with my father and stepmother, I observed and absorbed a lot—and that's really all I've ever said about the experience. And because of the love and respect I have for him, I won't write down here the things that happened, which, once committed to the page, would affect my father even more.

On some fundamental gut level, I somehow knew I shouldn't complain. I was a ten-year-old girl trapped out of sight, yet I understood that the best thing I could do was simply to remain silent. To this day, I haven't told my father these stories about Rita. Even as a kid it seemed clear that the best way to escape this situation was just to soldier on until this temporary situation was finally over. *This isn't forever*, I reminded myself. *This will be over soon.*

But when my stepmother attempted to obstruct communication with my mother, I simply couldn't stand by in silence. As young as I was, I knew I had to speak up, and right then and there, I gave Rita a piece of my mind.

"I heard you," I railed. "I heard when you told my mom that I wasn't here. Mark my words: if you ever do that again, I swear that I'll scream my lungs out until the police get here! Don't you ever dare lie to my mother again."

When my mother called the next day, I ran to the phone, trembling from head to toe, barely managing to form words. "Please don't do it, Mom! Don't let Rita adopt me. Don't give me away. Don't give me to her."

My mother and I spoke to each other in Albanian, so it seemed I could speak freely even with Rita standing right there.

"Trust me," my mother said. "I have no intention of giving you away. Eduard is and always will be your father, and I'm the only one who will ever be your mom."

That was the closest I ever came to revealing the misery I was experiencing in Switzerland. My mother knew me well enough to realize that I must have been extremely unhappy to speak so, with such desperation, with Rita hovering in the room.

"Don't worry, my light," she assured me. "I'll be there."

My mother was rattled when she hung up the phone. She feared that Rita might punish me when my father went out of town. She wondered what she could do from so far away to make sure I was okay. Of course, she, too, felt utterly helpless.

Making matters even worse, even though my mother and I spoke a brisk Albanian that Rita would never be able to understand, Rita had set up a tape recorder near the telephone so she could replay the conversation for my father when he came home and find out what my mother and I had said.

When my father heard the recording, he was, unsurprisingly, very upset—but it wasn't Rita he was angry with; he was angry with me. "Why are you behaving this way, Angela?" he yelled. "Do you want to go back to Albania and spend your life there, in poverty? Is that what you want?"

"Yes, Dad. I want to be poor," I retorted. "I don't care what I am, as long as I'm with Mom."

Not only was I so far from my mother, now I couldn't even enjoy the comfort of her voice. I knew Rita would record us; she would always record us. "Please send me back," I pleaded with my father. "That's all I'll ever ask of you. Please don't make me stay here."

Tears filled my eyes, and my father was deeply moved. Tears began to stream down his cheeks, too. He loved me; I knew he loved me. But Rita was unmoved by his rare display of emotion. It's amazing the way she could look at me with such disgust in the very same moments she demanded to take over my custody.

To be honest, there was something of an elephant in the room. There had long been a festering tension between my mother and Rita. It was a conflict about territory, it seems, more than jealousy, a resentment Rita had harbored but never bothered to communicate to my mom. I certainly knew nothing about it at the time, and even though my mother knew the backstory, she had no idea that Rita carried such a grudge and that the consequences of it would cause a domino effect throughout decades.

When my mother withdrew her asylum application—an act that prevented her from reentering Switzerland for five years—she had no idea that just two years later she'd find herself concerned about my health and determined to see a pediatrician in Switzerland.

At the time, health care was deplorable in Albania, and just in case I was found to have a serious condition (I didn't!), she wanted to make sure I had access to proper medical intervention.

She made an impassioned plea to the Swiss authorities to allow her entry despite the five-year banishment. When her application was approved, she and I flew to Switzerland, planning to return to Albania as soon as I cleared my checkups.

By this time, my father and Rita were already married, but my mother was determined not to let them know of our impending arrival or any of our plans. We were heading for Widen, Switzerland, a municipality in the district of Bremgarten, in the canton of Aargau, to live with a large family of eight (five children and their parents and paternal uncle), originally from Kosovo. They were friends of Blerti's, and Mom knew and trusted them. Shefget, their patriarch, paid for our flights; my mother certainly didn't have the funds. We were so grateful for his generosity and to have that place of refuge.

After a couple of visits and routine tests, the doctor gave me a clean bill of health. All the while, my father knew nothing of our presence in the country, but his name and address appeared on my doctor's bill. When the bill arrived at his house, my mom and I were already back in Albania.

Rita was particularly incensed by the assumption that my father would pay the charges. For one thing, my father had no idea what these charges were for. He tried unsuccessfully to reach Mom at the Shkodër post office, and then he appealed to Grandma Angelina to find out what had gone on.

Angelina wasn't pleased when my mother explained. "You should have *at least* let Eduard know that you and Angela were in Switzerland. Why didn't you at least tell *me*?"

"Because I knew in my gut that Rita would never consent to pay for Angela's medical visit," my mother said. "Would you have preferred that we settled for subpar medical standards? Doesn't he share the responsibility for seeing that she receives proper care?"

The truth is that when my parents divorced, my father left my mother and me with no money at all, and up until this point, my mother had never asked for or expected so much as a dime. She supported us alone and never made a peep to complain. The pediatrician in Switzerland was the one thing she wanted for me that she couldn't afford—and he could. It was necessary, and she was sure my father would agree.

"Of course!" Angelina nodded. "And I agree that Eduard must take financial responsibility. I'm just saying that you could have informed him of your trip."

Now that the trip was complete and my good health was confirmed, it was easier to imagine how the trip might've been handled differently, but in the moment, the travel complications and medical concerns were more than enough to think about. I can understand my mother's decision to avoid adding my father's new wife into the equation.

"You know I'm always on your side," Angelina said, offering my mother the warmest sort of hug. "And my son knows this too. I told him myself."

It seemed the matter was resolved, but it wasn't—at least it wasn't for Rita. For her, there was a completely unknown complex of emotions roiling beneath the surface of this one medical bill, but my mother didn't know any of that. The only thing my mother felt was the relief that everything was fine. And I knew my father loved me whether or not Rita resented this.

Perhaps part of her motivation to adopt me was simply an effort to get my father to sever his ties with my mother once and for all.

I cannot purport to understand what made Rita treat me as she did, but there I was in Switzerland, alone with her for hours each afternoon, a prisoner in that apartment, in a sort of solitary confinement for a significant stretch of time every single day. She offered no warmth, and she constricted the warmth I was able to give and receive, as she recorded the conversations I had with anyone back home. My grandmothers and aunts would call, and Rita would press RECORD. "Your mother is fine," they'd tell me. "Don't you worry at all."

They were forced to reassure me and placate my new mounting fears: ever since the adoption phone call and the subsequent recorded conversation with me, my mother hadn't called again. "Don't worry," said my aunts. "You'll see her soon," said my grandmothers. But now even her voice was out of reach.

"Where is she?" I begged. *Where are you?* I asked in my dreams each night.

Looking back, I can see the irony of the situation: I'd been forced from my home because of the threat that I'd be kidnapped, yet here I was—kidnapped.

VII

Pain with a Purpose

THE SEPARATION FROM HER CHILDREN WAS PAINFUL FOR MY MOTH-
ER, BUT IT WAS PAIN WITH A PURPOSE: BLERTI AND I WOULD BE
WAKING UP FAR FROM HER, BUT OUR HORIZONS WOULD BE BRIGHTER.
This was an inarguable fact—and the bleak future of Albania was on
display every day.

In January of 1997, Albanian citizens took to the streets in protest of the staggering losses so widely suffered in the Ponzi scheme
that many believed benefitted the government. The country's perva-
sive unrest was escalating to a civil war. My mother was grateful that
Blerti and I were at a safe distance from the deadly streets, but if she
planned to get out of Albania safely herself and reunite with me, it
was becoming ever clearer that she was going to have to move fast.

But the pressure she felt from Albania's warring streets was mild
compared to the urgency inspired by her conversation with my father
and Rita. Never would my mother sign over custody of me! The threat
weighed heavily on her, transforming her well-managed longing for
me into an overwhelming sort of sorrow. Prior to the demand that

she relinquish custody, my mother had been able to distract herself at work, throwing herself into her classes and students, keeping her longing at bay. Now, however, her longing was breaking through.

One day in late January, a student noticed her sorrow. "Why are you sad, Mrs. Nexhi?" the young girl asked.

"I sent my daughter to Switzerland," my mother replied, allowing her tears to flow.

"Oh, Mrs. Nexhi! Don't cry," the young girl said. "My brother, Bardhi, also lives in Switzerland. He's visiting us now. Do you want to meet him and see if he can help you?"

"I'd love to." My mother dried her eyes with a handkerchief as they arranged to have Bardhi come to meet my mom after school.

Bardhi was a charismatic twenty-three-year-old who arrived promptly and greeted my mother with great warmth. "It's so good to meet you, Mrs. Nexhi. My family speaks so highly of you as an educator and as a person. And my little sister adores you."

Mom smiled and proceeded to recount her story. "Do you believe that you can help me to obtain a visa?"

"I'm more than willing to try," Bardhi said. "But I must confess that I live and work illegally in Switzerland, so I'm obviously not well positioned to help you myself." He laughed lightly. "Nevertheless, I'll make every effort to find someone to help you secure a visa—someone to marry."

"But I don't wish to marry," my mother said. "I just want a visa—not a husband. I just need a visa to be with my daughter, Angela."

"I'll do my best," Bardhi tried to reassure her. "But you need to understand that you'll have to wait, yes? With all of the chaos here in Albania, the Swiss Embassy has canceled visas for a while."

"I understand," said my mother. What if she couldn't get to Switzerland? What would she do if she had to wait forever?

Indeed, my mother worried, but she has never been a person paralyzed by fear. She has always been remarkably adept at pulling herself together and pushing onward. "Bardhi," she said, training her mind on the future, "I'd like to ask something else of you, if I may. When you return to Switzerland, can you find out about housekeeping or cooking-related jobs for me there? I'm willing and able to do anything."

"I'll try," he said. "I'll do my best for you."

In addition to her extraordinary fortitude, my mother has also always had a knack for inspiring people to do their best—or at least to try.

...

Over the next few days, she installed a telephone in her parents' home and awaited the all-important phone call from Switzerland. She looked to the phone repeatedly and made herself quickly look away. *A watched phone never rings*, she told herself. But days passed without a call, suggesting that an unwatched phone might never ring either.

But one evening, the unwatched phone finally rang; Mom ran from the other room to answer it. When she heard Bardhi's voice, she almost jumped for joy.

"Listen, Nexhi. I found someone from Macedonia to assist with your visa application, but the process will be complicated," Bardhi said. "It's almost impossible to find a Swiss gentleman for this purpose, but it's up to you to decide what you wish to do."

My mother hoped to be connected directly with a Swiss citizen. "Thank you, Bardhi. I know that you're doing your best, but I don't think this is the answer I've been hoping for."

Once she set a goal, my mother was unstoppable in her efforts to achieve it, but she was worried about being stubborn in this situation: the odds weren't in her favor.

A few days later, she ran into her good friend Paulin, a photographer, who happened to be a friend of my father's, as well. He genuinely wanted to help my mother reunite with me. He suggested that she have a portrait taken and sent to an Italian agency in order to match her with a citizen there. My mother categorically refused; again she held out for a Swiss citizen.

As if to reward her for staying true to her goals, by pure happenstance, Bardhi called that evening. "A friend of mine knows a Swiss man willing to marry you because of your sterling reputation. I sang your praises!" he said. "Arnold Nussbaumer is a fifty-three-year-old divorcé, a great guy, and very hardworking."

My mother again protested about marrying.

"I explained that you don't want to marry," said Bardhi, "but my friend insisted that it's the only way."

My mother was starting to believe this was true.

"My friend is almost certain that you're going to like Arnold," Bardhi continued. "I can vouch for his good character—and the relationship will be good for both of you: you'll be reunited with your daughter, and Arnold Nussbaumer can find a good woman for himself."

"Why don't you call me again when you have more information," she said.

By that time, Bardhi had returned to Switzerland. He went with his friend Arif to Arnold's office to tell him about Mom. Arif was Arnold's business partner in a health insurance company, and Arif knew firsthand that Arnold had always been an incredible human being and philanthropist. It felt like an honor to play matchmaker for him.

"Arnold, you'll never guess what we found," Arif began jokingly. "It seems we've finally found a wife for you!"

Arnold looked up from his papers with curiosity.

"She's a wonderful Albanian woman," Arif said. "You'll love her."

"Albanian?" Arnold almost shouted. "Thanks, but no thanks."

He was adamant that he didn't want an Albanian wife. "I've met many couples from that region," Arnold said. "And the women all seem to shake my hand without looking me in the eye. I've always been troubled by that."

Bardhi jumped in to speak with passion on my mother's behalf. "That may be the case, Arnold, but you won't find that with Nexhi. She comes from one of the most civilized Albanian cities and she's extremely open-minded. She's a highly educated woman who works as a teacher and is beloved by her students and their families."

Arnold listened intently.

Bardhi and Arif had agreed that it was probably best not to mention my mother's goal of reuniting with me. Surely Arnold would prefer to think that he was of primary interest.

"Why don't we go for a drink?" Arnold suggested. "We can continue our conversation at the corner bar."

Bardhi was delighted; it seemed like a good sign that Arnold was willing to keep the conversation going. The three men walked to the bar and ordered their drinks.

Arnold sighed deeply. "What kind of woman is this Nexhi? How can she marry a man she hasn't ever met—a man she hasn't ever seen, for God's sake? And how can I marry her under such circumstances? It makes no sense to me," Arnold said, puzzling over the situation as he stirred his drink. "An arranged marriage definitely isn't what I've been hoping for."

Observing Arnold's skepticism, Bardhi sensed that it was probably best to tell Arnold the truth. Though he didn't know Arnold the way Arif did, Bardhi sensed that the man would be moved by my mother's longing to be reunited with her child. "There's more to this story," Bardhi began. "You see, Nexhi is divorced and has severed all ties with her ex-husband. Her ten-and-a-half-year-old little girl now lives with her father in Basel. Nexhi's most fervent wish is to reunite with her daughter."

Arnold coaxed his friend into telling the whole story, and after hearing the details, he was deeply moved. Although Arnold never had children, he adored them. He was taken by the story of the mother-daughter separation and the pain it caused. He'd always dreamt of having children of his own, but life had never presented the opportunity. *Why not reach out to this woman and assist her in this time of crisis?* he thought.

"The child is only ten and a half?" Arnold asked after a few moments' reflection. "What kind of people would deprive a little girl and her mother of living together?"

"You should know that Nexhi is beloved to so many in Albania, but only a Swiss citizen can pave her way here," Bardhi said.

But Arnold needed no more convincing. He was resolved to help my mother in any way he could. "Please give me her contact information and a photograph," Arnold said decisively.

"A photo? Why?" Arif asked in surprise.

"I want to see her face," Arnold said, "so that I can have a sense of the person I'm dealing with. From this distance, what other option is there?"

Bardhi was as thrilled to report this news as my mother was to hear it.

"I need all of your personal information," Bardhi explained over the phone. "Your phone number, place of birth, profession, et cetera—and one more thing: you must send a photo as well."

Mom could hardly believe her ears. It was funny the way opportunities could align and pave the path to one's future. After all, Paulin had just offered to take her photograph.

"Paulin!" she exclaimed, delighted as she stood at his front door. "I believe I've found the person to help secure my Swiss visa. It looks like I'll need a photo taken after all."

"Please, Nexhi. Quiet!" he cautioned. "Keep quiet about this. If the word spreads, you won't be going anywhere."

With a camera in hand, Paulin directed my mother to pose for her portrait. She was elegantly dressed in a black top and yellow jacket, her blonde curls cascading to her shoulders, but a wave of self-consciousness came over her as Paulin snapped her picture. There she was, courting a Swiss man in a yellow jacket as she posed against a bright red wall—not exactly fashion-forward. Nonetheless, she thanked her friend and went home. Without a second thought, she placed the photo in an envelope along with the detailed information that Bardhi had requested. She sent it off the same day.

And there was my mother once again—hopeful and waiting, just like me.

VIII

A Legacy of Longing

In Switzerland, I, too, was waiting for the phone to ring. It's difficult to explain how deeply I longed for my mother—to hear her voice, to smell her skin. Weeks had passed since her explosive call with Rita, and her voice hadn't materialized by phone ever since.

Every day presented the promise of a call—a possibility that gave me enough hope each morning to get out of bed. When the evening came without a word from my mom, I felt forlorn in a way no child should experience.

I'm being punished, I thought. *I must have done something horribly wrong somewhere along the way.* I replayed each and every wrongdoing I could recall. Had I been unfriendly to a classmate? Had I been rude to an adult? Had I shown disrespect to any person, place, or thing? "I'm sorry, I'm sorry, I'm sorry." I whispered the words throughout the day and as I lay in bed each night.

I was barely ten years old and clinically depressed. I was ten years old and desperate for a sort of redemption. What else could I do? I was ten years old and I began to pray.

My mother, too, had spent a good deal of her childhood longing for a parent, I reminded myself. Not only had she gotten through it, she was able to look back on her childhood with a wistful nostalgia. Her parents had settled in Shkodër, and although they were poor, they melded with the Albanian population of the times, doing the most with what little they possessed. Despite the extreme hardship, my mother truly believes that she had the best formative years possible, and she mostly credits her father with that feeling of stability. My mother was Daddy's little girl in every way. Her father was her world. He understood her, and his love fulfilled her above all.

Each day after school, Grandpa Muho would talk to my mother about the goings-on in her life, and he would beam with pride as he heard reports of his vivacious, gifted daughter's progress. "She's so intelligent and passionate about learning," my mother's instructors would say. "She's a regular on our annual list of excellent students."

Then, suddenly, the relative normalcy of the family's routine was painfully disrupted. My mother had just turned eleven when her father was sent to Bulqize prison. As if he hadn't suffered enough in the war, Muho was—out of nowhere!—sentenced to twenty years in a labor camp in Bulqizë. The offense was more than a decade old. The crime: idealism.

While working as a post commander in Iballë, Pukë, Muho had patrolled the border. One afternoon, he observed someone trying to escape, and instead of following orders to shoot anyone who tried to cross, my grandfather felt a humanitarian compassion. He ordered the border patrol officers to hold their fire and allow the man to pass. "There was nothing I could do," he wrote in his incident report. "The individual managed to cross the border before we could see him." Those words put an end to the case—but only temporarily.

More than a decade later, the escapee my grandfather had spared returned to Albania. The man mistakenly believed that policies had changed; they hadn't and he was arrested as soon as he entered the country. During Secret Service interrogations, the man revealed that Border Patrol had freely allowed his passage. When the authorities discovered that my grandfather had been serving as post commander at the time, he was arrested and imprisoned—by the very party on whose name he took an oath. "I swear on the Communist Party's idealism!" He often declared this when emphasizing a point or to demonstrate his sincerity.

When she received word of her husband's arrest, Grandma Dava fainted. With six mouths to feed (the youngest just seven months old) and without any financial resources other than her husband's income, she felt adrift in an ocean of sorrow and helplessness, facing a very uncertain future. What would happen to Muho—her rock, protector, and source of sustenance?

As for my mother, the eldest child, her characteristic internal joy became dampened by Grandma's roller-coaster emotions and panic attacks.

I know my mother longed for her father. I know she missed his presence in her life every single day. Yet her monthly visits to the prison made the reality of their circumstances all the more vivid and, at times, nearly unbearable. My mother was twelve when she first accompanied Dava to see Muho and bring him some food.

Like all of his fellow prisoners, Muho engaged in hard labor; but when he wasn't working, he'd stay in the visiting rooms, informing prisoners when guests arrived. So beloved was my grandfather that when his fellow prisoners received food from their families, they'd invariably give a portion to Muho for his wife and six children (five daughters and one son). Every four weeks during their visits, Muho would be the one bestowing foodstuffs to his visiting family rather than the reverse. Ironically, even as a prisoner, my good-natured, selfless grandfather managed to feed his family rather than waiting for them in order to be fed.

Due to their communist leanings, his parents and siblings shied away, seeking to avoid incrimination and a blemished reputation.

His wife and children were his only visitors. As for Dava, she never ceased to love her husband, but at the same time, she was angry. "You've destroyed our family!" she would wail. She began to look for work to support the family, but because of Muho's status as a political prisoner, she was not hirable. In effect, the entire family was considered traitorous—a criminal element in their own country.

My mother took to doing housework and did her best to adapt to her mother's tirades. Her opinion of her father never changed, and she simply couldn't understand why the authorities had taken him into custody. In her mind, he was—and he ever would remain— her confidante, best friend, and supporter. My mother longed for him—as I longed for her from Switzerland and as she longed for me. Perhaps this was yet another sort of genetic family trait, an inheritance of longing.

When it came to writing letters to Muho in prison, my grandmother, who was illiterate, deferred to my mother to complete the task.

"Nexhi, listen to me and write my exact words to your father," Grandma would say. "Do you understand?"

My mother would nod obediently as her mother began to dictate:

"Our children are growing up in the poorest of conditions. You have ruined our lives. Nexhmije feels hopeless. She cannot go to the library because of you. All I could give the children today was some dry bread and water, and even that was hard to provide since my salary is not enough to support them."

Not wanting to cause her father more grief than he already had to bear, my mother took liberties with the letter's contents:

Dear Muho,

We are doing well, and the children are growing up in good health. Please don't worry about us. I've found a job, and we get by. The children are going to school, and Nexhi goes to the library every day and continues to earn high marks.

When my mother finished writing each letter, her mother would say, "Now read what you wrote."

Struggling to recall her mother's dictation, my mother would improvise: "'Dear Muho, I hope you are well. We are managing and doing our best, and I have found a job.'"

"What? I never said that!" Dava would fly off into a rage.

"Don't worry, Mami. I'll correct what I wrote," my mother would reply, trying to temper her mother's wrath. When Dava got angry, sometimes she'd lash out at her children in the form of corporal punishment. My mother once revealed that her siblings endured such outbursts and physical abuse even more often than she did.

Yet despite her mother's insistence, the little girl who would become my mother never changed a word of those letters. Revealing any hint of despair to her father would have caused him enormous anguish, and my mother loved him far too much to take that risk.

This little girl with the beautiful green eyes would stop at nothing for her father's peace of mind; she would even sacrifice her own well-being. *I can let Mami be angry at me and sad about life, but Daddy's heart must never break*, she told herself, and she longed for him and waited—forever it seemed. She studied hard and earned good grades. She hoped and waited for her father to return.

At long last, when my mother was in her senior year of high school, Muho was finally rescued, courtesy of his wartime ally Kadri Hazbiu, with whom he'd fought against fascism in the Second World War. By then, Kadri had risen to a position in the government's Labor Party, which is how he came to be visiting the jail where Muho was held. When he visited the jail and found Muho in it, he was absolutely outraged.

"What in the world are you doing here, Muho?" Kadri said, in shock. "You're a model citizen!"

Muho could hardly believe his eyes. "My good friend," he managed to utter. "Are you really here?" Filled with emotion, Muho could hardly speak. He embraced his friend. Muho was just eighteen when they'd fought together; it was overwhelming to think about everything that had happened since then. My grandfather sank into a chair and began to cry.

Kadri placed a comforting hand on his shoulder. "You shouldn't be here," he said. "You've done nothing wrong. You fought valiantly for your country. You're a true patriot, and I promise I'll do whatever I can to help you."

Kadri made good on that promise, and Grandpa Muho was released in a month's time. Instead of twenty years, his sentence was commuted to six. "Go home to your children!" his friend said, his voice full of compassion.

Grandpa Muho was suddenly free. He was gaunt and worn from stress and sleepless nights, but when he arrived at the family's front door, my mother flew into his arms, sobbing and clinging to him with every ounce of her strength, as if she would never let go.

"Father, is it really you?" my mother said, her heart swelling with joy, relief, and gratitude.

That night, as the family went to sleep, they decided not to retreat to their separate beds. Instead, they spread out sheets and blankets on the floor so that they could be together, hugging Muho, delighted to hold each other closely through the night.

"You're here," my mother whispered to herself all night. "Dreams come true; you're here. You're really here."

When I imagined my mother appearing, as Muho had, at the door in Zürich, I felt a physical relief, as if I'd been deprived of oxygen for so long and was finally able to breathe. In my father's apartment in Switzerland, I spent many nights in my bed imagining just such a feeling.

IX

The Obstacle Course

WHEN BARDHI RECEIVED MY MOTHER'S PACKAGE, HE BROUGHT IT IMMEDIATELY TO ARNOLD NUSSBAUMER'S OFFICE AND ANXIOUSLY AWAITED ARNOLD'S REACTION.

Arnold held my mother's photograph in his hand and smiled. "Is this the woman you told me about? Nexhmije, with the little girl?"

"Yes," Bardhi said. "That's Nexhi."

In truth, Arnold was immediately taken with the natural grace and warmth in my mother's face, though he chuckled at the portrait's amateurish clashing colors. "Who would take a photo of this woman in a yellow jacket against this red wall?" he asked.

Arnold had already resolved to help my mother, even though some of his Albanian Macedonian friends had warned him of a potential scheme. "What if she's not really a divorced woman, after all?" they cautioned him. "What if her husband is here in Switzerland and she's just trying to reunite with him?"

Despite their concerns, Arnold would not be swayed. He was as clever as he was wise, as discerning as he was good-hearted. He had scoured the Internet for news of Albania, researching the turmoil plaguing our country. "Look," he said. "Albania is in the midst of a civil war. I don't know who Nexhi is or what her ulterior motives might be, but I believe Bardhi's claim that she's desperate to reunite with her daughter. I truly want to help her and I'm able to do it. How can I not?"

From all that he'd read about Albania's turmoil, he understood that it was entirely possible that he might end up saving her life.

That day, the three men, Arnold, Arif, and Bardhi, went to the embassy to apply for my mother's visa only to be met with disappointment. "I'm sorry," said an official working at the service counter. "We've ceased granting visas to Albanians."

"How is this possible?" Arnold protested. "I can't just leave my fiancée there! Her life is at risk merely being in that country."

"Oh! I'm sorry I misunderstood," said the clerk, handing Arnold a visa application. "If this woman is your fiancée, of course you can apply."

When Bardhi called my mother that evening to share the good news, she was beside herself with joy at the prospect of seeing me, and she couldn't believe her good fortune. "Bardhi," she said, "thank you from the bottom of my heart. Truly. I'll never forget you."

...

Two weeks later, my mother received a package. It was pouring rain, and she walked into my grandparents' apartment drenched and carrying a huge envelope. My mother was late returning from work, and Grandma Dava had been worried sick. Despite being soaked from head to toe, Mom wasn't thinking at all about her comfort or appearance. It didn't even occur to her to set down the envelope and change into something dry. Instead she stood at the kitchen table—the same table at which we'd sat when she first told me I'd be moving to Switzerland—and she opened the envelope, her hands trembling with excitement.

Inside, she found a packet of documents—all of the paperwork her own emigration would require. There was also a postcard depicting the beautiful Swiss Alps, along with Arnold Nussbaumer's business card.

My mother could hardly breathe. "Mom! My Swiss visa," she said, shaking with joy and enthusiasm.

The postcard was written in Italian. Bardhi had informed Arnold that my mother didn't speak German, but understood Italian fairly well, which was definitely an overstatement. She showed Grandma Dava the photograph on the front of it and the handwritten note on the other side.

> *Cara Nexhi,*
>
> *Come stai? Spero che tu possa venire in Svizzera questo sabato, perché domenica parto per le montagne Svizzere. Io vado a sciare li ogni anno, e non voglio perdere l'occasione quest'anno. Spero tanto che tu possa farcela.*
>
> *Arnold Nussbaumer*

What Bardhi had told Arnold about Mom's moderate aptitude for Italian wasn't exactly true. In fact, she knew only a few words and phrases that she learned from watching the Italian channels everyone in Albania received on their TVs. Suffice it to say, she wasn't sure she fully understood the message, and this was no time for misunderstandings. Mom ran to the next-door neighbor who was far more fluent and was able to translate the postcard.

> *Dear Nexhi,*
>
> *How are you? I hope you can come to Switzerland this Saturday, because on Sunday I leave for the Swiss mountains. I go skiing there every year, and I don't want to miss the chance this year. I very much hope you can make it.*
>
> *Arnold Nussbaumer*

When she heard what Arnold had written, she nearly leapt with excitement. *This was real. She was practically on her way.* But a mild panic promptly began to set in, tempering her giddy delight.

Saturday! It was so soon! Though she'd been married before and she'd been to Switzerland before, this plan was forcing her to navigate uncharted territory. She hardly knew what to do or think. All she knew was that she was about to take a huge step, forging ahead alone in her midforties, leaving her family and—civil war or not—her beloved nation in order to step into a strange life with a complete stranger. Of course, she was driven to see me; nothing would eradicate that desire, but waves of fear came over her nonetheless. She started to worry over unforeseen obstacles—expenses, language barriers, whether or not she'd be able to pull this off.

She sat with her friend, calming her nerves over a cup of coffee. Once again, my mother managed to collect herself, rally her courage, and press on.

She went to the neighborhood post office and dialed the first number on the business card.

"Halo," a sweet male voice answered on the other end of the line.

"Io sono Nexhi,"[3] she said.

"Ma quale Nexhi?"[4] the gentleman asked.

Mom was at a loss for words—her heightened anxiety was constricting her already limited grasp of Italian, forcing even the basics out of reach. "Albania, Albania!" she blurted.

A clumsy start to a relationship, indeed, but Arnold immediately understood that language limitations were at play, and he was deeply touched by my mother's warmth and enthusiasm.

They continued their brief conversation, my mother offering her tangled Italian and Arnold patiently deciphering her words. He wanted to make sure there was absolutely no confusion about the

---

[3] *"I'm Nexhi."*

[4] *"Which Nexhi?"*

next steps she should take. "Take the documents to the capital," he said. "And prepare them so that you can leave soon."

The next day, Mom and her sister took the bus to Tirana and went straight to the Swiss Embassy. An official named Bledar took her passport and the documents that Arnold had sent.

"Are you receiving assistance from a Swiss man?" Bledar asked.

"Yes, sir," Mom replied, feeling a bit uneasy.

Bledar extended his hand to take my mother's passport, explaining that she could retrieve it in a couple of days. "Come back on Thursday," he said. "And just fax your plane ticket to us by then."

My mother froze. There was no way she could gather the money for a plane ticket by then—certainly not on her meager teacher's salary. She and her sister had planned to ask for loans, but even with family, friends, and neighbors chipping in, she had only accumulated half the airfare. Doubt began to creep in once again, but that night, out of the blue, Arnold called to inquire about her progress.

"Things went well in Tirana," she explained. "But I must purchase the plane ticket."

"What are you waiting for?" Arnold asked. "Go ahead, Nexhi, buy it!"

My mother was moved by his enthusiasm, but she was embarrassed to tell him the truth. Instead, she made up a story about a temporary closure at her bank that, for the time being, made it impossible to access the funds. "As soon as circumstances change, I'll let you know," she assured Arnold. She hated to lie, but in the moment, she felt she had no other choice.

When Arnold provided his colleagues with this update, all of them began to laugh.

"What's so funny?" Arnold asked in dismay. He felt enormous compassion for my mother already. He was quick to defend this woman he'd not yet met. "The poor woman has to wait until the bank reopens to buy her ticket, and who knows how long that will take?"

"What bank? What money? There's no way she could've saved enough for a plane ticket," Arif explained. "Nexhi is just a schoolteacher. No matter how hard she works, in Albania it's unlikely that she's able to earn anything more than sixty Swiss francs."

"What? Sixty Swiss francs?" Arnold asked, amazed.

Arif nodded. "She's probably just buying time until her friends and family can gather the money."

The next day, Friday, Arnold bought a plane ticket for my mother and sent it by fax to the Swiss Embassy. Fortunately, her Italian-speaking neighbor was able to rush to the phone and translate Arnold's news.

"What?" my mother asked. It was nearly impossible to believe that this person she'd never even met had bought her a plane ticket that cost more than she could possibly make in a year. "Thank you," she said, though she could hardly breathe. "Oh, thank you!" Relief coursed through her body. With this plane ticket, Arnold—a complete stranger!—had bought my mother hope and a future, lifting her above every hurdle that stood between us. "Tell him I will repay him someday," she insisted of her neighbor. "He must know that I'll repay him someday."

Though she didn't know it at the time, my mother would, indeed, repay Arnold years later, helping him clear the myriad hurdles that arose between him and his future as he battled cancer. My mother took on the role of physician, researcher, dietitian, and rehabilitation expert as she miraculously nursed him to complete remission, much to the amazement of his doctors. In the moment, however, the only thing my mother could do was weep with gratitude and pack her suitcase.

She gathered the bare necessities, just a few articles of clothing. She managed to purchase a new suit for the occasion—a short black skirt and a black and white jacket that she would wear on her trip. An elegant winter coat and shoes finished off her attire. The next morning, she dressed meticulously for her departure, applied her makeup, and loosened her beautiful blonde curls. "Nexhi, you're a sight for sore eyes," said her sister Edi, who was accompanying Mom to Tirana.

They would pick up my mother's ticket and her visa at the embassy and then head directly to the airport in time for Mom to catch her three p.m. flight. She was on her way!

At the embassy, Bledar, the same official she'd met last time, rose to greet her, addressing her by name.

"Hello, Mrs. Nexhi. How are you?"

"Eager to retrieve my visa," she said. "Excited to get on that plane."

"I don't know how to tell you this, madam," Bledar said with sorrow. "But you were denied the visa."

My mother turned as white as a ghost. "Why? I did everything precisely as instructed."

"The Swiss government won't allow you to enter the country," Bledar explained. "Your file has been marked with a red X."

"What is going on?" she shouted. "Why is the world conspiring to keep me from my daughter?"

Out of nowhere, the Consul appeared, apparently startled by my mother's cries. He repeated Bledar's explanation that the Swiss government had denied her entry. "Perhaps in the future, Herr Nussbaumer can rectify the situation, but for now, our hands are tied."

Every time it seemed that she was on her way, another roadblock appeared in her path. My mother couldn't help but sob. Her heart was breaking, her body trembled, and she felt hopeless, once again.

"Listen," Bledar said with a look of compassion. "Here is the Consul's phone number. Why don't you tell Herr Nussbaumer to call him immediately and see if anything can be done? Why don't you leave your passport here—and hurry. There isn't very much time before that flight!"

"Oh, Bledar!" My mother was overtaken by a wave of gratitude. For each obstacle she encountered, it seemed a guardian angel would suddenly appear.

She placed the passport back on the table between them.

"Don't worry," Edi said reassuringly. "We'll find a way."

...

Every hour of this day presented a new challenge. When one lives in comfort, one forgets how challenging the smallest tasks become.

In order to call Arnold, they'd have to get to the post office, which was far away and they were pressed for time. Without money for a taxi, there was no choice but to walk, taking turns carrying my mom's tiny suitcase. "Come on. Let's keep going." Edi offered encouragement along the way.

When they arrived at the post office—windblown and exhausted—my mother called Arnold's number, but Arif was the one to answer the phone.

"Arnold's out making preparations for your arrival," Arif said. "You'll be here this evening, right?"

My mother explained the situation, and the next hurdle presented itself in her path: Arif would find Arnold as soon as possible—but he needed a phone number for Arnold to call.

This time Edi's quick thinking saved the day. She had a friend in Tirana and offered Arif that number. Without any assurance that this friend would be home and able to receive the call, Mom and Edi could only hope for the best as they dashed to this woman's house.

Fortunately, Edi's friend was at home. She greeted them warmly and promised to keep her phone line free until the much-anticipated call from Arnold came in.

"At last! Where have you been?" my mother replied. Hours had passed. She'd been choking back tears as she imagined missing her flight. "Please help. I can't lose my daughter."

The moment my mother learned that her visa had been denied, she'd been shocked. *Why on earth would the Swiss government ban my entry?* she'd wondered. *Why on earth would anyone thwart the reunion of mother and child? Who would do such a thing?*

As soon as my mother had this thought, she also had the answer. Rita was the only person on earth, it seemed, who wanted to break my mother and me apart.

The Swiss government certainly wouldn't ban my mother's entry because she refused to relinquish custody of me, but, my mother realized, maybe Rita had done something else. She remembered the bill from the Swiss pediatrician years earlier. In her mind, my mother could hear Angelina's voice explaining how angry Rita had been when my father received the bill. Could that be the problem?

She explained the situation to Arnold. "I should've notified him beforehand, but the only thing on my mind was getting Angela quality care."

Arnold was profoundly moved. He recognized that my mother was in a desperate situation and vowed to do whatever it would take to get her there. He told my mother not to worry and to stay by the phone. Then he sat back in his chair, drew in a deep breath, and dialed the Consul's personal phone number. The obstacles kept coming, but throughout the entire emotional roller-coaster ride, he was certain about my mother's integrity and her earnest desire to see me again. Not a hint of doubt ever entered the mind of this remarkable man.

"Sir, this is Arnold Nussbaumer calling from Switzerland. My fiancée has been denied her visa from the Swiss Embassy. I hope that you can inform me as to the reason. I've done everything possible to make the necessary preparations, and I don't believe that I've missed a step. Please help me to figure out what has gone wrong here."

"You see, Mr. Nussbaumer, the problem lies in the fact that Mrs. Nexhi's ex-husband and his present wife have filed a complaint, stating that she wants to enter the country with the intention of destroying their family. They also assert that when Mrs. Nexhi was last in Switzerland, she sent her ex-husband a pediatrician's bill without prior notice. These are serious allegations, Mr. Nussbaumer."

"Herr Konsul, I know about that bill, as my fiancée briefly mentioned it to me," Arnold said in a serious tone. "Are you punishing a devoted mother for ensuring proper medical care for her child? Surely, you are aware of the substandard medical conditions in Albania and the poverty that so many endure there. Nexhi is among those people. She simply couldn't afford to pay for the little girl's pediatric evaluation—while the girl's father certainly could. While it's true Nexhi should have notified her ex-husband in advance, she did not violate the law. I only regret that I didn't know her at the time, or this would never have happened, and I can guarantee that nothing remotely like this will ever occur again."

The Consul was moved even before Arnold began to elaborate on his relationship with my mother.

"We met in Italy, and I want to marry her when she arrives in Switzerland," Arnold said. "Please, Herr Konsul, give us this chance to be happy. I don't know what Nexhi's ex-husband's motivation was in sending that complaint letter, but I do know that her desire to come to Switzerland is driven by her desire to see her daughter and to find happiness here with me."

Moved by Arnold's plea, the Consul gave in. "I can arrange for you a three-month tourist visa," he explained. "Tell your fiancée that her plane leaves at three p.m. She really must hurry!"

By the time the phone rang at Edi's friend's house, my mother's entire body ached with stress and anxiety, but as soon as Arnold delivered the good news, she felt as if all her strength had miraculously returned. She could hardly find the words to thank him. "Molte gracie, Signore Nussbaumer,"[5] she mumbled, though as she and her sister grabbed the small suitcase and began running toward the embassy, she thought, *This man is my guardian angel. How can I ever thank this guardian angel?*

The embassy was far, and the airport farther. Since they couldn't afford a cab, my mother flagged down a random car passing by. "Sir, I don't have any money with me, so I can't pay you, but can you please take us to the Swiss Embassy and then to the airport?" Her hair was wind-blown and tousled; tears were still welling in her eyes.

"Yes," the driver replied. "I'm happy to help." He beckoned Mom and Edi into his car.

Who were these angels clearing my mother's path to me? She

---

[5] *"Thank you very much, Mr. Nussbaumer."*

thanked the driver repeatedly. "I'll never forget your kindness," she said—and she hasn't.

Upon entering the embassy, Mom saw Bledar, the officer who'd given her the Consul's phone number. She took his hands in hers and kissed them. "I'll never forget you or what you've done for me," she said.

"It's my pleasure," Bledar said. "I'll always remember your devotion to your daughter. I wish you a safe trip, and please give little Angela my love."

With her heart pounding and barely enough time to catch her flight, my mother arrived at the airport terminal only to find another obstacle separating her from her plane. She discovered she had to pay a small boarding tax, but without any money, it made no difference how minor the cost.

It was too much to bear!

"Officer, help!" she cried, summoning a law enforcement official to her side. "I'm not carrying any money, and I must get on that plane. I promise you—I really do—that I'll pay the fee as soon as I return to Albania."

Compassion overtook the officer's face, and he allowed my mother to board.

"I'll never forget your face," she said. "And, you'll see, I really will pay the fee upon my return."

Then she turned to her sister, embraced her, and quickly said farewell. In a daze, she walked down the aisle of the plane, with the same tiny suitcase she'd been toting around all day. She was taking with her only the barest necessities. When she reached her seat, she slumped into it, closed her eyes, and wiped her forehead with a handkerchief. In just a few hours, she'd be standing once again on foreign soil, without any money and with tremendous gratitude to a man she was expected to marry but had never met. "Angela, Angela, Angela!" my mother suddenly cried. Concerned, the stewardess came running down the aisle, bringing my mother a glass of water and a pill to reduce her stress. Still, my mother continued to call out my name.

X

What Have I Done?

THE SOUND OF MY MOTHER'S VOICE CALLING MY NAME HAS ALWAYS SOMEHOW RESONATED IN MY SOUL. *Angela! Angela!* I can hear it in my mind pronounced precisely in my mother's accent. *Angela! Angela! I'll be right behind you!* The thought of these words had begun to taunt me as I lay sleepless in bed at night.

I confess that my faith in Mom's promise had begun to fade and was being supplanted by profound disappointment. By the end of February 1997, I hadn't seen my mother in three months and had not heard her voice in two. I had no idea that she had arrived in Switzerland. All I knew was that it seemed she'd disappeared.

"She's okay," said my aunts.

"She loves you; we all love you," said my grandmothers.

"Maybe she no longer cares to speak with you," Rita suggested. "Or maybe she's gone off to Italy or Greece to pursue her own life."

Deep inside, I knew this wasn't true, but these thoughts nagged at me, as if they'd lodged under my skin and had begun to itch. I knew my mother loved me with all her heart and soul, but her absence and now this sustained silence had given rise to anxiety and frustration. I roamed from room to room, but I had no outlet for this fear and frustration.

It was starting to seem clear that I was being punished for something, but for what, I had no idea. *What had I done? What could I ever have done to deserve this?*

Somewhere along the line, I began pulling out my own hair. Sometimes I did this as I roamed; more often I just sat in a sort of fugue, tugging and yanking, one strand at a time. Perhaps that brief bleat of sensation in my scalp helped me—for just a second at a time—feel something other than sorrow.

"Oh, my God!" Rita said. "There's hair *everywhere!*"

She and my father chided me and pulled out the vacuum, but neither of them seemed to notice the bald spot on my head, its diameter expanding daily, along with my sorrow.

XI

Strange and Immediate Comfort

THE FLIGHT FROM ALBANIA TO SWITZERLAND WAS ONLY TWO
HOURS, BUT MY MOTHER'S JOURNEY THAT DAY SEEMED NEARLY
ENDLESS. It was hard to believe that just that morning she and
Edi had been running to and from the embassy, propelled by panic
and toting Mom's tiny suitcase all the while, unsure until that last
minute that she'd actually be going anywhere.

But there she was, landing in Zürich so exhausted it felt as if
she'd been traveling for days. As she disembarked, she realized that
she wasn't quite sure whose face she should be searching for in the
crowd. She had no one but me on her mind: *Angela, Angela, my
light, my love.* This played like a soundtrack in her head every day,
and so she was jolted out of her exhausted reverie by the sight of
Bardhi, who was standing beside an elegant man.

Of course, my mother had never even seen Arnold Nussbaumer
before, but all of the grace, compassion, and the quiet command he'd
managed to convey over the phone were evident in the gentleman
she saw standing there. As their eyes met, my mother felt a sense

of familiarity that seemed nearly impossible to find with a stranger.

Given the intensity of the experience they'd navigated together, it wasn't entirely surprising that Arnold felt it too. "There she is," Arnold said, turning to Bardhi and pointing in my mother's direction. "That's her, isn't it? The woman in the suit."

"That's Nexhi, all right," Bardhi said, waving at my mom.

Arnold says he'll never forget that moment and the way his heart skipped a beat.

Bardhi made the introductions, and Arnold greeted my mother warmly with a kiss on both cheeks. My mother, in turn, expressed deep gratitude for his kindness. Bardhi brokered a brief exchange of getting-to-know-you chit-chat, but noting the ease with which the two conversed, he left them to set out on their way.

My mother was fatigued beyond belief and still fixated on finding me, while Arnold was doing his best to remain mindful of the maternal force that had driven my mother to Switzerland. Bardhi had made it clear to Arnold that my mother wasn't interested in marriage; she was only interested in me. And Arnold had made it clear to Bardhi that he had no romantic expectations; my mother's story moved him, and he was helping out because he could.

If you'd asked either of them in that moment if they had romantic designs on one another, both would've responded with an emphatic *No!* But ask them about it now and both will readily admit that as they stood side by side that day at the airport both felt a giddy mixture of anticipation, trepidation, and joy—and both now understand that it was love at first sight.

...

Arnold's Zürich neighborhood was quaint, quiet, and welcoming. A gentleman, Arnold stepped around the car to let Mom out of the car; he carried her suitcase to his front door and welcomed her inside.

Compared to the houses in Albania, Arnold's house was a

mansion. The front door opened into an airy, spacious living room with a balcony. Arnold gave her the grand tour: the master bedroom, the office, the guest room. The entire space was immaculately clean and airy, though my mother noticed right away that it lacked a woman's touch.

He invited my mother to choose any one of the rooms to call her own.

"I'll choose the one with the library," my mother said. "I love being among books."

"As you wish," Arnold replied, taking her suitcase to the room.

When my mother noticed a miniature replica of a plow hanging on the wall, she couldn't help but ask Arnold about it. "Mr. Nussbaumer," she began, "I'm curious to know where you found that plow. In Albania we've lived in poverty for centuries, and plows and peasants are a common sight—but in Switzerland? It seems there wouldn't be so many plows around."

Arnold explained that a friend from Kosovo had given him the plow as a gift.

My mother found a strange and immediate comfort in that plow, in the fact that Arnold had a friend from Kosovo, and that he seemed to be at least somewhat familiar with her world.

"Don't worry, Nexhi," Arnold said as if sensing some lingering unrest. "You're safe with me here."

Later, after my mother had changed and they sat down for dinner, they took turns telling personal life stories. My mother has always been talkative—especially when nervous. She allowed herself to slip into an easy cordiality, as if she hadn't been driven to Switzerland with a singular intent.

It was only after Arnold presented to my mother his plans for them to spend the next ten days in the Alps that she finally spoke up. "That sounds so wonderful," my mother said politely. "But I'm really quite anxious to get to Angela in Basel."

"Of course," Arnold said. "But I think we need to spend at least a bit of time making a good show for the Consul at the Swiss Embassy in Tirana. He was very sympathetic to the notion of you being my fiancée, and I think it's important to establish some support of our purported relationship before you stir the pot with your ex-husband and his wife."

"I understand, Arnold," my mother said. "But I must see my daughter."

My mother was so grateful to Arnold. She already felt a surprising connection to him—and a significant affection for him—but more than any Prince Charming who might step into her life, my mother had been longing for me.

How could I possibly come all the way to Switzerland, my mother thought, *and not see Angela right away?*

"I can imagine how you feel, Nexhi, but the trip will only be for ten days," he said. "I've already told my friends at the ski resort that you'll be traveling with me. You have no contacts here in Zürich, and I don't want to leave you in the house alone."

My mother sighed and made her resistance clear, but Arnold kept steering my mother to the Alps. She trusted him—he'd helped her get this far already—but after all the difficulty getting into Switzerland, why on earth would he think she'd want to spend her first ten days at a mountain resort? She didn't even ski. "I'd like to call her at least," my mother said. "Angela should know that I'm here. That we're not nearly so far apart as we've been."

Arnold reached across the table and kindly gave my mother's hand a squeeze. "Nexhi, I can imagine what you must be feeling. If I were you—and if I were lucky enough to have a daughter—I wouldn't be able to relax until I could hold her in my arms or hear her voice just to be sure that she was all right," he said, speaking with patience and compassion. "But you're simply going to have to wait."

Arnold explained that my mother had no choice but to lie low for a while. Not only had Rita red-flagged my mother, she'd asserted that Mom was a threat to her family. This was a serious charge! If Eduard or Rita learned that my mother was in Switzerland, they might report her to the authorities—a risk that could result in speedy deportation.

The short-term satisfaction of making immediate contact with me wasn't worth the risk of the long-term consequences. "You've come so far, Nexhi, it would be foolish to sabotage it now," Arnold said. "I promise you'll see each other soon enough. In the meantime, come see the Alps and relax."

My mother had been worrying and scrambling for months; the past twenty-four hours alone couldn't have been more stressful and exhausting. "There are worse places to wait this out than in the Alps," Arnold said kindly. My mother knew this was true. Ten days in the Swiss Alps was hardly a horrible thing.

···

On the way to the Alps, Arnold stopped to pick up his best friend's wife, Francoise, who would help my mom pick out some skiing clothes at the mall.

"I don't even know how to ski," my mother laughed. "You don't have to buy all these clothes for me."

"Whether or not you ski doesn't matter; you're going to need warmer things to wear. It's quite cold in the mountains," Arnold insisted.

My mother and Francoise took an instant liking to one another. Francoise helped Mom pick out a skiing outfit and hiking boots, some warm sweaters, and a nightgown.

The drive out of town brought them through the most beautiful scenery, the likes of which my mother could never have dreamed—forests and valleys and vistas all covered with snow.

They stopped for lunch before getting on the cable car to the chalet.

The restaurant was small and cozy; the lunchtime portions generous. The food must have been delicious because Arnold savored every morsel. He'd nearly cleaned his plate when he looked up to notice that my mother was only drinking coffee, completely ignoring her meal.

"Aren't you hungry?" he asked. "You didn't eat a bite at home either."

"I'm fine," she replied softly.

Culturally speaking, it is typically Albanian to shy away from food the first time it is offered by anyone but family and the closest of friends. My mom told me that when they were in the restaurant, Arnold ordered for himself, but didn't ask her again if she was hungry. But my mother was hungry and planned to order food after being asked several times, but she was only asked once. After Arnold ate, he asked my mother if she would like some coffee, and she immediately said "yes," knowing that she would not be asked a second time.

Beyond the desire to not impose, my mother was still feeling somewhat shy and uncomfortable in the strange limbo of being near me but not with me.

As they rode the cable car up the mountain, my mother was in awe. The view was breathtaking, with all of the chalets brightly illuminated against the snowy terrain. She felt as though she were in a fairyland. *What is Angela having for lunch?* she wondered. *Is she warm enough? Is she sleeping well at night?*

...

They spent the evening at a nearby restaurant with Arnold's brother, Roland; Ruth, his wife; their children; and another couple. Once they were settled at their table, Arnold told everyone the reason for my mother's trip to Switzerland, all the while glancing and smiling reassuringly in her direction. She was grateful that he introduced my name at the table. I was on my mother's mind, and she found it comforting to learn that I was on his mind too.

Everyone spoke German, so my mother couldn't follow the dinnertime conversation, yet instead of feeling alienated and left out, my mother felt comfortable and safe merely being in Arnold's presence. When the evening ended, the two returned to the chalet.

The next morning, Arnold and his friends headed off to ski. He gave my mother three hundred francs to spend on sightseeing or snacks until they all reconvened for lunch.

Three hundred francs! It was the equivalent of four months' salary back home. It was difficult to get her head around the idea that here in Switzerland such an amount might all be spent before lunch.

She wandered around, taking in the sights, wishing she were sharing them with me. Arnold had given her a cell phone, and she pulled it from her purse, resisting the temptation to call me at Dad's home. Rita was likely to call the authorities if she knew my mother was in Switzerland, and the offense she had charged was serious enough that the authorities would, indeed, respond.

"Give it a little time," Arnold had said. "I promise we'll come up with a plan."

The fresh mountain air was as invigorating as the magnificent beauty all around. The snow-capped mountains rose like majestic castles in the sky, towering over the landscape of trees and little chalets strewn about, all of them glowing with the warmth of a fireplace and the cheer of the people inside.

Back at the chalet that evening, my mother and Arnold returned to the chalet, chilled by crisp air and exhilarated by such a glorious day. Their room was furnished with two separate single beds; they'd slept separated by yards the night before. "Maybe we should push them together to keep warmer?" Arnold said as they prepared for bed.

In other circumstances—and in other company—my mother would have been unnerved by such a question. She had just arrived and barely knew this man. Though she was free-spirited in many ways, she also worried about etiquette and what other people would think—but not this time. Not with Arnold. There was an undeniable attraction between them, and her soul allowed itself to surrender.

She nodded in agreement, and they joined their beds together, uniting in passion and paradise. At last, my mother felt she'd found a secure place in the world, and after his years of bachelorhood, Arnold felt the same way. His heart was as big as the universe; he'd just been waiting for The One to come along. Owing to pure chance—or destiny, or fate, or divine intervention—there she was, in his arms, newly arrived from a war-torn nation.

On their last night in the Alps, he held her warmly. She'd never felt quite so safe in her life. He cautioned her that his company in Zürich kept him very busy; he wouldn't have time to spend with her as he did here in the Alps. He wouldn't be around as much as he'd like to help ease her adjustment. But he wanted to remind her that his focus had always been—and remained—on making a difference in her life and helping fulfill her goal of reuniting with me. My mother wasn't worried. It had already become abundantly clear that both of them were saving each other.

XII

True Bedtime Stories

My mother had landed in Zürich, met the man she'd ulti-mately marry, explored the Alps, and made new friends—and I had no idea that she and I were in the same country. Had I known she was so close, perhaps I wouldn't have been spending so much time daydreaming about Albania.

My Albania! How I missed the streets—full of kids year round. During the long, hot summers, the grown-ups would join us outside, enjoying the evening breeze as they sat on stoops or on dining chairs lugged down to the sidewalk from their sweltering apartments. With no one to talk to, I spent a lot of time telling myself family stories: the one about my mother's birth; my grandparents' taboo marriage; my beloved brother, Blerti, banishing me to the balcony when the smell of my diaper was more than he could take. The more vividly I could picture the stories, the more vividly I could conjure the family love I'd left behind.

Once upon a time, after the war, Grandpa Muho traveled to Iballë, Pukë, an old village in Northern Albania. One afternoon in

1948, he happened to pass through a village called Gojan i Vogël. Mounted on horseback and clad in distinguished military garb, he took a moment to pause and enjoy the fresh, clean air. Pulling slightly on the reins, he descended into a valley, where a group of girls was herding sheep.

Noticing him, the young girls hid their heads in their scarves—all except for the sixteen-year-old, black-haired beauty. The girl glanced at Muho and smiled, and as he looked into her sparkling brown eyes, he felt an instant connection. *She's remarkable!* he thought.

Intrigued, Muho resolved to pass by the village every day in hopes of seeing the girl out herding sheep. Sometimes, she would look up and smile, and sometimes the two engaged in friendly conversation—even though girls in those days were forbidden from speaking to males outside the family circle, but even as a little girl Grandma Dava was already something of a free thinker.

Despite the Albanian government's attempt to obliterate the custom, children were pledged in arranged marriages, often before they were even born. Dava grew up in a devoutly Catholic family, and she'd been promised to a playmate when she was ten years old—but six years later, a charismatic war hero rode his horse into Dava's life and changed it forever. She harvested figs from the fruit trees surrounding her house and presented them to Muho in a basket.

Such a sweet gesture! Unfortunately, her mother, Prena, witnessed the exchange and stormed out of the house, incensed that Dava had disgraced the family. "You know you shouldn't be offering anything to any man!" she ranted. "Not even to a post commander!"

Her tirade continued as she grabbed her daughter by the arm, took her into the house, beat her severely, and threw a wooden stool at her, breaking her front teeth. With a bruised face and swollen lips, Dava could barely move.

When Muho heard about what had happened, he confronted Prena. "Listen," he said. "I'll put you in jail for what you've done to your daughter."

"I don't care about your threats," Prena railed. "My daughter will have nothing to do with you!"

With all that Muho had been through in the war, he certainly wasn't about to be intimidated by Prena.

But after this heated exchange Prena kept her daughter hostage in the house. Dava had to stop attending school and could no longer herd sheep. Secretly, she and Muho exchanged messages through her friends, and one day he asked her to run away with him. Two horses would be waiting at an appointed hour at a specific spot in the village, and if she agreed, she was to meet him there in the dead of night.

The plan was set, and without breathing a word to anyone, Dava went to sleep on the floor with her siblings, just as she would on any other night, except that she was anxiously awaiting the right moment to leave. Without looking back, Grandma Dava went to meet her future husband in the village, where four heavily armed soldiers were awaiting her on horseback. The two went straight to the municipal offices in Pukë and announced to the authorities that, by mutual consent, Muho had taken a Catholic girl from her home and intended to marry her, even though, prior to her birth, she had been promised in marriage to another. The commanding officer respected and praised the decision, decrying the Communist policies that prohibited interfaith marriages between Catholics and Muslims.[6]

After addressing these matters, the couple traveled to Muho's home in Shkodër, where they were greeted by his mother, Sultana, and his four younger siblings (two sisters, Hasije and Nafije, and two brothers, Hamdi and Ahmet).

"Who is this beautiful girl?" they inquired.

Muho couldn't summon the courage to tell his family the truth—at least, not at first. "She's my friend's sister and has come to study here in Shkodër."

Satisfied with the story, the family welcomed and befriended Dava, but when they learned that she was Catholic and that Muho

---

[6] *Albania is constitutionally a secular nation and was the first atheist country in the world.*

planned to marry her, the family went into a collective rage. Sultana descended into a state of despair, beating herself until her legs turned blue and screaming aloud, "*Kuku, kuku!*[7] What have you done to our family?"

At the time, a Muslim-Catholic marriage was practically unheard of, and the news caused a stir across the entire neighborhood. My grandparents left and settled in Pukë because my grandfather accepted a job there as a post officer. Although they were poor, they melded with the Albanian population of the time, doing the most with what little they possessed.

Whenever a man took away a daughter—especially one promised to a marriage before birth—the old and vengeful Albanian Kanuni customs dictated the killing of the first fourteen-year-old male in the new couple's bloodline. Fortunately, Grandma Dava's family didn't try to find her or make contact after she left home, but Grandma Dava's children would've been safe anyway. She and Muho had five girls in a row, the first of which was my mother. By the time Dava finally had a son, the threat had lifted as Grandma Dava's family had finally reconciled with her.

...

Once upon a time, there was a snowy winter day in Pukë. It was December 5, 1950, and Grandma Dava had gone into labor. Her contractions were very close and intense from the start. With his trusted horse as their only transport, Grandpa Muho had no choice but to hoist Dava into the saddle—but no sooner had he done so than Dava could no longer defer the inevitable.

With her husband's careful assistance, she lay in the middle of the street and gave birth. My grandfather suddenly became her obstetrician, cutting the umbilical cord of their first child.

---

[7] *"Oh no! Oh no!"*

Since the weather was far too blustery to travel to the hospital, they cradled their daughter in their arms and went back inside the house. Necessity and inventiveness won the day—a perfectly appropriate beginning to my mother's life.

Nexhmije's initial birth name, Jeta (life), was Catholic. Not surprisingly, when Sultana, my paternal great-grandmother, heard about this decision, she became so angry that she nearly fainted. "I will die because of this!" She was inconsolable. "My son, not only have you married a Catholic woman, but you also gave the child a Catholic name. This is going to kill me!"

"What do you want me to do, Mother?" Muho asked in a measured tone.

"Name her Nexhmije," Sultana insisted.

And so the little girl was called Nexhi—by everyone but Prena, Dava's mother, who insisted on calling her by her Catholic name.

Her birth in the winter street was my mother's initial test of resilience—one of many to come—proving to everyone again and again that adversity and survival are flipsides of the same coin.

…

Once upon a time, in Shkodër, there was a baby girl surrounded by a bustling, busy family. Her parents, grandparents, aunts, and cousins adored her—as did her older half brother, Blerti. He was twelve years old when she was born and so fascinated by the tiny creature that was his sister, he'd often run upstairs from the street when he was playing with friends for no other reason but to see her face.

"What is it, Blerti?" their mother would ask. "You went outside just a few minutes ago."

"I wanted to take a quick peek at baby Angela," he'd say like a doting little father.

When their mother went to work, Blerti was more than happy to take care of the baby for the day. Their mother always made sure to leave the baby in a clean diaper, but one day the baby's digestive system was determined to make itself known.

Poor Blerti didn't know how to tend to a baby's hygiene! Odors began to fill the apartment, and desperate times called for desperate measures. The young boy took his soiled infant sister out onto the balcony, where the air was crisp and fresh. At the time, it seemed to him like a really fine idea! The baby shivered in the cold all day until their mom came home.

"Where's Angela?" their mother asked upon her return.

"She pooped, and the odor was so bad I thought it would be best to take her outside." Blerti smiled with pride, impressed by his own problem-solving skills. He gestured toward the balcony door, and the mother rushed outside in horror.

"Oh, my heart," said the mother. She lifted the baby girl in her arms and held her tightly to her chest. She rocked the baby with urgency and worry, pressing her cheek against the baby's head. The mother inhaled deeply, again and again, breathing in the scent of her little girl, which was as vital to the mother's well-being as oxygen itself. "My heart! My beautiful heart!"

The mother was near tears as she rushed the baby girl inside. "You need a warm bath. You need a thousand kisses and blankets. You need to feel warm and loved, Angela. You should always feel that way."

The baby girl and her whole world were at peace in the mother's arms. Indeed, she did feel warm and loved. Indeed, her mother would forever make her feel this way.

...

In Switzerland, I woke at five a.m. and ate warm yogurt every day. I pulled out my hair and paced from room to room. I prayed like Grandma Dava taught me. And I told myself true stories.

XIII

Master Class

ARNOLD WAS RIGHT: THEIR WHIRLWIND ROMANCE WOULD NOT BE
THE SAME WHEN HE AND MOTHER RETURNED TO ZÜRICH. Arnold
worked long days, and my mother was at something of a loss without him.

She had virtually no friends in the country, she couldn't speak
the language, and she didn't have a job. Her world seemed to stop,
as though she'd stepped off the earth and landed on an entirely
different planet.

At first, my mother set about keeping busy with cooking, ironing,
cleaning, window-washing, and taking on various laborious tasks to
pass the time and distract her mind.

When Arnold called during the day to ask how she was, she replied, "I'm fine—cooking, cleaning, and making your lunch."

"But I never come home for lunch, Nexhi," he said. "Why don't
you go out for a walk, my love? Don't forget: there's a lake just fifteen
minutes from home."

My mother could hardly get her head around Arnold's kindness and compassion. Neither of her ex-husbands ever would've encouraged her to get outside merely to enjoy herself. Xhafer and Eduard were each, by turns, too jealous and too demanding.

Without knowing more about my mother's first husbands—Xhafer, Blerti's father, and Eduard, mine—it seems nearly impossible to understand how otherworldly this idle time was for my mother and just how miraculous Arnold seemed from the get-go.

My mother was just twenty years old when she met her first husband. Though she hadn't yet graduated from university, she approached the administration with fiery enthusiasm. "Is there any possibility of working here as a teacher?" she asked, determined to help her family make ends meet.

Despite the administrators' skepticism, my mother passed the necessary exams and began to work at Shkodër University as its youngest teacher. Fairly close in age to her students, she still wore her hair in two long, thick braids, which made her look especially youthful, but she quickly earned respect as a teacher. With all the beauty of youth and the competence of adulthood, she met Xhafer.

She was at a neighborhood tailor shop being fitted for a new dress when she noticed a tall, handsome, young man standing out on the street. He was watching her through the shop window. She briefly met his gaze, and he flashed his most charming smile. Though she quickly turned her attention to the mirror and the tailor pinning her new dress, she and the young man on the street continued exchanging glances through the window throughout the entire fitting.

Xhafer Ceprati came from Vlorë, on the southeastern coast of the Adriatic Sea, from which his educated, wealthy family had fled from Communism. He was so enchanted with my mother that he returned each day to wait in front of the shop, hoping she'd return to pick up the garment and he'd have the chance to see her again. When, finally, she arrived, Xhafer was standing in front of the shop waiting for her.

This time, it was the tailor who watched through the window as my mother and Xhafer chatted on the sidewalk and then parted ways, the budding romance between them already apparent.

The tailor was the first—of many—to object to this romance.

"If you marry that man," the tailor warned, "it'll ruin your life." He cautioned my mother about this particular young man, who, the tailor knew, had fled political persecution with his family. But this warning hardly registered with my mother; her own father, Muho, had also been a target of political persecution, and he was the most wonderful man she'd ever known.

"You're otherwise so smart and mature," said the tailor. "Your goal should be to finish your studies and become a good teacher. Forget about this man; he'll never be able to find firm footing in this society."

But each time she ran into Xhafer, my mother's feelings for him grew. He often appeared beside her—in the neighborhood or at school—ready to walk her home. There was a fundamental decency to his character that she genuinely admired, and soon it was official: they were dating.

My mother's family was as displeased as the tailor. Of course, in Muho's eyes there wasn't a man in Albania who was good enough for my mother, but the urgency of his warnings actually gave my mother pause. "You have to graduate before marrying," Muho insisted. "Besides, what can this man offer you? You're far more learned. You've read more books than anyone in town!"

But my mother's affection for Xhafer was only growing deeper, and in spite of her family's protests, she continued to date the man who'd captured her heart. Hadn't her own parents defied their elders in order to be together?

One day Muho spotted my mother as she prepared to set off on her bicycle, and he decided to join her to make his final appeal. The two went together to the Grand Café, leaving their bikes locked outside. Muho ordered a single shot of raki (moonshine) for himself and one for his daughter.

"I'm going to beg you one last time," he said. "It doesn't matter that Xhafer's father was educated or that his family once had wealth. Your intellect far surpasses his, and he'll never be able to fully understand you."

"But he's a good person," my mother countered. "I'm twenty years old, and he's twenty-three, and we're ready to start a new life together."

I can imagine how adamant my mother must have been: She was smart, beautiful, and on the brink of starting her career. She had no reason at all to doubt herself.

Grandpa Muho sighed. "Are you pregnant?" he asked—awkwardness be damned! "If you are, just tell me. You don't have to marry that man just to raise the child; I'll raise the child."

"I'm not pregnant," said my mother—and she wasn't.

Muho shook his head, finally understanding that there was nothing he could do. "Mark my words: you may end up marrying him, but you won't end up with him for long."

The date for the engagement party was set. It would take place just two weeks later—and these weeks marked some of the happiest times of my mother's young life. She loved Xhafer for his tenderness, thoughtfulness, and his charm; he never failed to pay her a compliment or to consider her well-being. However, immediately after the party, things began to change.

Xhafer couldn't seem to stop himself from criticizing my mother's parents. He could be cutting and underhanded, and there was practically nothing that Dava or Muho could do that didn't grate on Xhafer's nerves—a significant problem as he was living in their house.

At a certain point prior to the wedding, my mother grew frustrated at Xhafer's insulting treatment of her parents. Turning to Muho, she confessed, "I don't want to marry him anymore. I don't feel good about the marriage."

Grandma Dava was worried about the impact a broken engagement might have on my mother's reputation, but Grandpa Muho knew better. "It's better to break up now, while you're still unmarried," he reasoned. "Once you have children, it will just be harder to leave him. This is your home—as it always will be. And right now, you have a choice."

When my mother confronted Xhafer about calling off their engagement, he was irate. He ranted about her family, accusing my mother of not having a mind of her own. The power of attraction can be wielded in insidious ways, and Xhafer somehow managed to make my mother lose her resolve and start second-guessing herself. *Maybe Xhafer is right*, she thought. *Maybe my crazy family really is to blame for our problems.*

When Xhafer grabbed hold of my mother's bicycle to keep her from riding away, something inside my mother softened, and later that day, when the two made love, my mother became pregnant. Though they had agreed from the start not to have children before marriage, it seemed in this instance that Xhafer had a strategy: if he got my mother pregnant, she couldn't leave him.

This accelerated my mother's plans for the wedding as she pushed to have the event as soon as possible, never telling her parents what motivated this urgency. Dressed in their most elegant attire, the couple arrived at City Hall to get their marriage certificate, when the fates presented one last obstacle—or one last chance to back out.

When Grandma Dava had escaped her parents' home to be with Muho, she hadn't thought to bring her birth certificate—which had prohibited the two from formally marrying. To retrieve the document, Dava would've had to return to her angry family, and that certainly wasn't an option. Despite the Communist law dictating that cohabiting couples had to marry, my grandparents just continued to live together and have a family, never making their union official. There had never been a consequence to this until now: my mother couldn't get married unless her parents were officially married as well.

"You can get married at the same time, if you wish," the official at City Hall suggested.

"There's no way I'm sharing a wedding day with your parents," said Xhafer with disdain. "I told you that your family is *dhjakonar*."[8]

If only my mother had taken the opportunity to back out then!

Instead, the young couple decided to have a small, private celebration with family and friends a few days after Dava and Muho married. My mother wore a simple white dress. She looked radiant and wore a flower in her hair. The newlyweds moved back in with my grandparents, and three months after the wedding, my mother finally announced that she was pregnant. Though news of the impending birth inspired great joy, Xhafer's temper continued to flare in those small, crowded rooms.

Of course, everyone absolutely adored baby Blerti, gathering to dote on him during bath time, lavishing him with sweet-smelling soap as my mother sang lovingly to him. Such moments were pure joy—but they were consistently punctuated by Xhafer's frightening outbursts.

Xhafer worshipped his son and was an incredibly attentive father, but his jealous streak was profound. My mother had long tried to ignore it, but after Blerti's birth, it was impossible to avoid. Xhafer was convinced that my mother was somehow deceiving him. He resented her popularity, her professional success, and the ease with which she moved through the world. He simply could not accept that my mother's grace and charm never made her any less of a wife or a mother to his son.

Xhafer was also a germophobe—an obsession he clearly learned from his own parents, who would criticize my mother for her handling of her own baby. Xhafer frequently berated my mother, undermining her at every turn, assaulting her verbally and, ultimately, physically as well.

Muho and Dava urged my mother to divorce Xhafer on grounds of irreconcilable differences, but my mother was reluctant to take that step.

Xhafer ended up doing the filing himself, even as he continued

---

[8] *Poor; low class*

to live with my mother, under the same roof. Xhafer became increasingly volatile and harassing, trying to force himself on my mother and causing a scene as he ranted about how she denied his requests for intimacy. Neighbors began to stand in judgment of my mother—not Xhafer!—and eventually, with great courage, my mother picked up her son and left, moving in with her parents once again.

Then, a year later, after having no contact at all, my mother ran into Xhafer on the street. Despite everything they'd been through, it only took a moment of eye contact before they each felt a rekindling, the full force of their connection surfacing again. The two remarried in Vlorë and moved to Shkodër. Blerti was delighted to have both parents living together again, but Xhafer soon started in on his tirades again—and this time, my mother left for good.

...

She was miles away from that now. It was all eons ago. Now, as she strolled around the lake in Zürich, she felt so lucky to have met Arnold that she couldn't help but burst into tears.

That night, Arnold came home to a meal cooked for an army. Since she was used to serving a large family, my mother had cooked enough food for a month. There was no way the two of them could consume all of it, and having come from a country entrenched in poverty, throwing it out felt like a travesty. This commonplace dilemma forced each of them to redefine their customs and habits and the kinds of things they took for granted.

Above all, it was essential to my mother's well-being that she find something to occupy her mind. She certainly wasn't about to curl up and surrender her identity to a man. "I'm never going to thrive here without knowing the language," she said one afternoon, determined not to become languid and bored. "I'd like to take a German-language course."

Arnold looked up from his plate of *imam bayildi*, a popular eggplant dish from the Ottoman region that Mom had prepared for him. "A language course?" he said. "Learning a new language is remarkably ambitious for a woman with just a three-month tourist visa."

My mother was crestfallen. It was true that there was a time limit on the duration of her visit, but Arnold's casual reference to it made it seem as if he didn't mind that this also put a time limit on their relationship. She took a deep breath, trying to restrain her tears. "Yes, I know," she said. "But I want to make the most of my time here."

"It's an excellent idea," Arnold said. "A great way to spend your time. Let's enroll you right away."

Arnold researched language schools on the Internet, and the next day they set out to enroll Mom at a school located in the center of Zürich, more than seven tram stops from home.

She was eager to integrate herself into Swiss culture, and there was no better way to achieve this than to learn the language. Arnold made the arrangements and then translated the conversation for my mother into Italian. "Class starts this week. You'll just have to be here at eight thirty a.m."

"Okay," my mother said, but the city suddenly seemed larger as she wondered how she'd find her way to the school alone.

As if sensing her concern, Arnold offered his hand. "Don't worry," he said. "You'll just need to remember that your stop is at the Stampfenbachstrasse station."

Mom could barely say the word, and she certainly couldn't spell it. Arnold handed her a booklet of directions and various street maps. *My God, I have never seen anything like these signs and directions*, she thought, feeling perplexed and uncertain.

Two days later, and my mother was in launch mode—ready to take off early and arrive at her destination on time.

She grabbed a seat next to the tram's driver and asked him to inform her when they reached Stampfenbachstrasse station.

The passengers around her chatted or read the newspaper or

minded their own business, while my mother sat at the edge of her seat, scanning the signs through the windows: *Stampfenbachstrasse station? Stampfenbachstrasse station?*

As they approached each station, the driver made his customary announcements and Mom listened intently, worried she'd miss her stop, but in less than a half hour, she stepped from the tram and made her way to the language school. Breathing a deep sigh of relief upon her arrival, she headed straight to the administration office. "Classes don't start until eight thirty," the receptionist said, pointing to the clock.

After all that worry, she'd arrived early!

Perhaps it was a traveler's high—the morning's journey through unfamiliar streets—or maybe it was a rush of newfound independence, but my mother was excited to take in every sight and sound. Eventually she'd get used to her new environment, she told herself. She just had to pay attention and memorize landmarks so as not to lose her way. She waited eagerly for the instructor to step into the classroom, to crack open a new world for her as she learned an entirely different language.

"Ich heiße Helga Hilmer. Heute werdet ihr alle Deutsch lernen."[9] The instructor seemed efficient and precise, yet also warm and welcoming. As my mother sized her up for the first time, it was impossible to imagine the incredible impact Helga Hilmer would have on Mom's life.

"Entschuldigung, wie hießt du?"[10] Helga began.

When my mother's turn came to introduce herself, she ventured, "Ich bin Nexhmije Nussbaumer." Arnold had registered her with his surname, and this was the first time she identified herself this way. Somehow, the name sounded strangely comfortable. Before they'd met, she had no interest in getting married; any interest in Arnold had been driven strictly by her desire to reunite with me. Yet, now that they'd met and were so clearly falling in love with one another, she wondered how far he'd be willing to go in order to keep her in Zürich.

The class was four hours long, which had seemed like an eternity

---

[9] *"Today all of you will learn German."*

[10] *"Excuse me, what is your name?"*

when she first noted the schedule, but the time flew and my mother enjoyed every minute of it. Over the following days and weeks, she quickly emerged as one of the most devoted students. She enjoyed mingling with her fellow students, and sometimes after class they'd all grab lunch together at a nearby mall.

Now reasonably familiar with the Zürich streets, my mother would walk over to Arnold's office, where they'd spend the afternoon together, Mom learning to use Arnold's computer or studying her German diligently while Arnold worked.

Whenever she had trouble with her homework, she'd appeal to Arnold's Albanian Macedonian coworkers for help. They'd all managed to learn German out of sheer necessity, so they could communicate smoothly—but grammar was quite another matter. German verb conjugations could be maddeningly tricky; even Arnold himself could not explain some of the rules. Mom forged ahead through irregular verbs and tenses, and her proficiency quickly resulted in high exam grades. Her instructor, Helga, was both pleased and amazed. "Nexhi, where are you from?" she asked one day.

"I come from Albania," my mother said.

"Albania?" Helga exclaimed in surprise. "You're my second Albanian student, and I must say I marvel over the educational programs offered under the Communist regime. My Albanian and Russian students have always been the best in my class."

She noticed that a couple of her fellow students always sat behind her during exams, looking over her shoulder to copy her answers. One day, she offered to explain some grammatical rules, and both of the men were enthralled. "I haven't been able to understand at all until now, but when you explain, everything becomes clear!"

One day, Helga used the word *stein* in a sentence, and everyone looked baffled as Helga struggled to translate the word for stone. My mother understood what the teacher had said, and true to her lifelong impulse to share her knowledge, she asked to leave the room, returned with a stone from a nearby park, and showed it to the class. Everyone was delighted. None of her classmates would ever forget that word!

Soon, she was able to declare her profession in German. "Ich bin Lehrerin."[11] Helga recognized my mother as a kindred spirit—eager to learn and teach simultaneously.

Equipping herself with the native language, my mother began to feel she had a foothold in Swiss society. Getting a grasp on the city and its culture had seemed like such an impossibility when she arrived; now, with just this rudimentary command of the language, life in Switzerland suddenly seemed navigable. Arnold was thrilled to see her exuding such joy, and he assisted my mother in every way he could. "Ich bin stolz auf dich!"[12] he declared lovingly, and my mother ached to know what the word *stolz* signified.

When Arnold brought her an Albanian-German dictionary, the first thing she did was look up the word. *He's proud of me*, she realized, and she was elated.

Mom soon became a teacher's assistant in the master class, helping instruct the same students she'd begun learning with. Helga split the class in two, and Mom taught one of the groups. Some students specifically requested to be in her section. My mother was as effective as a teacher—and she was fun.

"What kind of 'help' does a verb actually need?" one student asked on the day the group was baffled by the concept of "helping verbs."

Mom was quick on her feet, readily offering a relevant analogy. "Consider me as something of a helping verb," she explained. "A smaller verb assisting the larger. I assist the teaching. Nexhi *is* teaching."

She was also building an excellent reputation among Helga's coworkers, who had heard about her language aptitude, her far-reaching curiosity, and her teaching skills. Consequently, Helga wanted to nurture her as much as possible and went so far as to have coffee with her after school and provide one-on-one instruction.

"It's very unusual for a teacher to take time to give individualized

---

[11] *"I am a teacher."*

[12] *"I am proud of you!"*

instruction to her students. You should feel honored," Arnold remarked when Mom told him about their meeting.

With a burgeoning command of the native language and a
reputation in Switzerland that went beyond whatever my father
and Rita might have to say, it seemed that it must be safe to contact
me by now. Would the government really toss her from the country
based exclusively on one woman's say-so?

"I'm serious," she said to Arnold. "I must see my Angela. Don't
ever forget that she's the real reason I came all this way."

Arnold tenderly stroked Mom's hair. "I haven't forgotten—but
I understand how important this is, and I don't want us to make
any missteps."

The Swiss Consul had been emphatic when he overrode my
mother's red-flagged file and granted her a visa. Arnold had giv-
en his word that my mother would steer clear of her ex-husband
and his new wife. "If they know you're in the country and call the
authorities, they have an obligation to get you out of Switzerland.
And this isn't anything that a quick call to the Consul can fix."

"But when?" she asked Arnold, overwhelmed with the magni-
tude of the consequences Arnold described. "My visa is only good
for one more month."

"Trust me," Arnold said. "I have a plan. I know how tempted
you must be to call Eduard's apartment, but you mustn't. Doing so
could place you at great risk—even if you call from an unknown
phone number, Eduard can find out where you are. I hope you trust
me. Do you?" Arnold asked.

She did. The situation was agonizing. She'd left a war-torn
country to feel war-torn inside. *Angela. Angela. Angela.* My name
had become a sort of prayer, a song perpetually running through her
mind. But she had come to understand that everything Arnold said
and did was from the heart. His concern for her was real, and so was
his compassion. "Do I trust you?" she repeated. "Yes. I absolutely do."

XIV

Voices on the Radio

IT WAS MARCH; IT WAS APRIL; IT WAS NEARLY MAY.

Beyond the cement wall just outside my window, I could see the seasons changing, mostly from the light and color of the sky.

I woke up to my father's exercises and got out of bed at seven a.m. Brushed teeth. Made bed. I turned on the radio, paced back and forth, and tugged out strands of my hair. I ate a warm yogurt, told myself family stories, and waited through another day.

At some point, I found an Italian-German dictionary on my father's shelf. It was almost impossible to live in Albania without picking up some Italian just from watching TV. You could be six years old and fairly fluent just from watching cartoons. I had a little knowledge of the language from tuning in to fairy tales, so I tried to teach myself German by first translating Albanian to the Italian I'd picked from watching Cinderella and Snow White.

There was little comfort in the fact that I wasn't the only one growing frustrated with my mother's disappearance. My father and Rita were still waiting for her to sign over custody. "This is your life until she signs those papers," my father would shrug. If his goal was to get me to the point of begging my mom to sign just so I could go to school, it wasn't going to work; my mother never called, so how could I beg?

The radio became my constant companion, connecting me to the outside world—and helping me conjure my own future. I loved Craig David, and I dreamed of being part of the same world as my favorite artists. How many ten-year-olds have that much time to visualize their future?

Once upon a time, there was an Albanian girl separated from her mother and trapped in a Basel apartment. She got through each day by listening to the radio, which became the soundtrack of her dreams. She had no friends, no activities, no school, no teachers, and nothing to do—*at least not for now*, she told herself. One day she would turn eighteen and she'd be gone quicker than a shot. If she could just wait until then, she could go anywhere on earth. She could go to New York City and become a model. She could join her favorite singers in their favorite city. They became her teachers and mentors and friends; all these far-off singers who inspired her and kept her company became much more than just voices on the radio.

XV

Sacrifice, Accommodation, and Bliss

Sorrow and longing bore heavily on my mother's heart and spirit. As time passed, she began to brood ever more deeply over her circumstances and the thought of what seemed like our far-off reunion. She became so despondent that she stopped going to language classes. Helga, her instructor, expressed concern over her state of mind.

"I'll be fine," my mother said.

She'd recently been feeling guilty about nearly every aspect of her life in Switzerland: she was living so comfortably while her family was in financial distress; she was enjoying her romance with Arnold, but she wasn't getting any closer to reuniting with me.

"Nexhi, I am so proud of your progress," said Arnold as he handed Mom a check to pay for her third month of class. "It's incredible how quickly you've begun to communicate freely in German. It's hard to believe that you've been here for only two months."

My mother smiled and thanked Arnold. She'd never before been the one to deliver the check, so Arnold instructed Mom on how to complete the necessary paperwork. It was only as she slipped the check into the enrollment envelope that she finally noticed the amount. She was shocked; each month of her language lessons had cost over eight hundred fifty Swiss francs.

"Oh, my goodness, Arnold! Is this the price for just one month?"

"Don't worry," he said. "It's not that much."

When my mother converted the figure to Albanian lek, she almost fainted.

As she walked to the post office to send off her enrollment, the class tuition haunted her. She couldn't get it off her mind. She thought about her father, who was ill at home with prostate cancer, and she thought about her mother's meager pension, which could barely feed the family. She knew her mother's sisters Edi and Teuta were struggling as well—Edi unemployed, and Teuta paralyzed. The universe felt out of balance. My mother couldn't bring herself to remit such a substantial check when her impoverished family struggled to survive. She simply couldn't do it, and so she turned around and headed back home.

"I've decided to homeschool myself this month," she explained to Arnold, handing him his check. "I'm far ahead of the other students, and I have a good idea of how to proceed with my studies."

"Are you sure, Nexhi?" Arnold asked, looking at Mom with a mixture of admiration and doubt.

"Most definitely."

Arnold said, "Du bist alt genug um deine eigenen Entschei-dungen zu treffen."[13]

Mom laughed. "Mehr als alt genug."[14]

She began to study from home, and predictably, Helga called to inquire about her absence from class. "Is everything all right?" Helga asked. "Things just aren't the same without my star student."

"It's not about you, Helga," my mother assured her teacher. "I just became aware of the expense, and it didn't feel right to enroll."

[13] *"You are old enough to make your own decisions."*

[14] *"More than old enough."*

"Nexhi, the price is standard in this country," said Helga. "And you must know that this is one of the nation's best language schools. Besides, you're taking an intensive course, so the cost is a bit higher than a regular classes."

Mom explained the significant difference that even a fraction of that amount could make in sustaining her family back in Albania. "It doesn't seem right to indulge in language classes when my family is struggling over necessities."

My mother had made up her mind.

That evening, Arnold returned home from work in a somber, reflective mood. "Nexhi," he said, "Helga called me. I'm so sorry that your family is in so much distress. I hadn't been aware that conditions were so dire there. My Albanian coworkers confirmed the economic crisis—but you must understand that you don't have to do without because your family lacks money. You can't sacrifice yourself for anyone—not even your family or your children. If you don't care for yourself, how can you expect to be of help to anybody else?"

Arnold took my mother's hand. "Nexhi, my parents made similar sacrifices for my siblings and me, but they were misguided. Unless you establish yourself here in Switzerland, learn the language, and prosper, it will be impossible for you to secure their well-being. Everything will be lost if you neglect yourself."

"I understand, Arnold," my mother said. "And I'm deeply grateful for your wisdom and concern, but I must insist on doing without the course this month. I've been a teacher all my life, and I assure you that I'll be fine."

"You can try your methods for a month," Arnold said decisively. "But after that, you're going back to school."

Next month, my mother thought. *By next month I'll be gone.*

In spite of the obvious comforts of her new life, Mom became disheartened by the passage of time. She was so happy with Arnold, but she couldn't bear to think that their relationship had distracted her from seeing or speaking with me. I know that the pain in her heart was agonizing because I know it was in mine. Imagine us—so near, yet so far, both of us wondering and waiting, struggling in the agony of each other's absence. Memories of Albania and our little apartment on the fifth floor played like a movie in my head—just as they played in hers, I'd later learn. Surely we must've spent some of the same nights overwhelmed with frustration and longing, crying ourselves to sleep as if the distance between us were far greater than an hour's car ride.

My mother's sorrow wasn't lost on Arnold. Later that week he took my mother for lunch by the lake near their home. He looked at the menu, ordered, and waited for Mom to do the same. He then launched a conversation that would forever change our lives.

"First of all, Nexhi," he began, "I want to thank you for keeping your promise throughout your time in Switzerland. You've restrained yourself from contacting Angela, even though this has caused you enormous pain. I understand how difficult it has been for you to be without your precious girl, but the stakes are simply too high to go about reuniting in a foolhardy way." Arnold cleared his throat.

As she looked at him, Mom could practically hear her own heartbeat. Her mind raced and anticipation was driving tears to her eyes. "Go on," she said in a small voice.

"Dear Nexhi," he said, "I've been thinking, how would you feel about living here in Zürich?"

"I'd love it," my mother said.

"Are you saying that only because our marriage will grant you access to Angela?" He looked down for a moment, suddenly shy. "Or would you truly wish to live here anyway?"

He didn't dare to utter the words, but my mother understood the subtext. What he was asking was, *Will you stay here for me?*

"I would love to live in Switzerland because of my daughter, of course, and also because of everything else that I've been so lucky to find here. But what can I do? You know that my visa expires in just a few weeks." My mother reached out to caress Arnold's hand.

With intense respect and love evident on his face, Arnold asked my mother, "Will you marry me?"

My mother's heart skipped a beat as she blurted the one word Arnold yearned to hear: "Yes!"

Mother jumped with joy, and Arnold laughed aloud. Arnold later confessed this was born not just of happiness but from the sincerity of my mother's response, as if she wanted to say, *What took you so long to ask?*

Arnold stood and took my mother in his arms, allowing his head to rest on her shoulder. At that moment, the chaos of the world seemed to retreat, as if they were the only two people on the planet. They'd come together to find me, not love, but what a miracle it was that their union would bring both at the same time.

…

Brimming with joy, Mom ran home to call her sister Edi and tell her the news.

Edi was elated. "Oh, Nexhi! I'm so happy for you." Tears were streaming down her sister's cheeks.

The last time my mother and Edi had seen each other had been the day they'd navigated the obstacle course of getting my mother and her paperwork onto the plane. With a wedding on the horizon and all the bureaucracy that it would require, the obstacle course had begun yet again.

There were documents my mother needed to procure from Albania, but with the country in the throes of civil war and the government's administrative offices seized by gangs, there was little chance of getting them—even with Edi's tireless help.

Fortunately, the Consul at the Swiss Embassy in Albania instantly remembered Arnold as soon as he called.

"How is everything going, sir?" the Consul asked.

"We are well, Herr Konsul, thank you. Though we're having some difficulty obtaining the required documentation to get married here in Switzerland. We're quite desperate to have the issue resolved, and for that reason, once again, I've turned to you," Arnold said earnestly.

"Please don't worry, my friend. Just send nine hundred francs to the Swiss Embassy in Albania, and we'll make sure that one of our employees prepares the documents and sends them right away. At long last you and Mrs. Nexhi will be married." The Consul's voice resonated with joy.

"I cannot thank you enough, Herr Konsul. You've been more than kind."

Just two days later, the required documents arrived by mail. Holding hands, my mom and Arnold ran, like two adolescents, to the city hall. "Time is running out!" they said, almost in unison.

Their excitement was not without limits, however. According to Swiss law, a couple's impending marriage had to be published in the newspaper for a week to provide an opportunity for people to come forward and express opposition. Naturally, Mom and Arnold held their breath for an entire week, wondering if my father and Rita would see the ad and ruin their plans.

Fortunately, the worst did not occur, but the Swiss authorities were on Mom's back, warning her that she had to leave the country before her visa expired. Alone at home when the order arrived, she panicked and called Arnold at work, frantic about what to do next. As usual, Arnold comforted her, reassuring her that she had nothing to fear and that the authorities wouldn't be knocking on their door.

Less than a week later, my mother and Arnold were officially married, with Mom deciding to keep both the Ibrahimi and Nussbaumer surnames. "No one can respect you if you don't have your own identity, and Ibrahimi is my identity," she declared.

My mother's heart was thrumming as she and Arnold left their ceremony. If Mom had any fear that her new husband might be offended that she was more excited to celebrate their marriage with a phone call to me than an intimate evening with him, Arnold put that fear to rest before they'd even made it home. "Nothing could be more wonderful than finalizing our union," he said. "Except for the fact that our marriage also means that you're free to call Angela at long last."

My mother was trembling, weak in the knees with her heart aflutter, as if every kind of love was surging through her all at once. "Go ahead!" Arnold said, as he unlocked the front door.

This was the moment my mother had been waiting for—the culmination of so much sacrifice and so much restraint. How many times had she thought about picking up the phone, just dialing despite Arnold's warnings, hoping I might pick up and that she'd get to hear my voice, even if she said nothing before hanging up the phone. She was nearly light-headed in anticipation, so she took a deep breath, collecting herself yet again before pressing on, and she dialed my father's number.

Rita, of course, was the one to answer—a fact that inspired my mother to flex her new language skills. How dare anyone try to take her daughter away! No one was more competent than my mother; she could do anything—listen up! She was already fluent in German.

"Ich bin Nexhi, Angela's Mutter,"[15] she said.

"Wer sind Sie?"[16] Rita asked in a shocked tone.

To Rita's disbelief, Mom continued speaking in German. "Nexhi. Ich heiße Nexhi, und ich möchte mit meiner Tochter sprechen."[17]

"From where are you calling?" Rita asked.

"From Zürich," said my mother.

"When did you arrive?" Rita sounded as if she already felt somehow threatened.

"I've been here for a while," said my mother. "While it's a pleasure speaking with you, Rita, the reason I'm calling is to speak with my daughter."

"Hold on, Nexhi."

[15] *"This is Nexhi, Angela's mother."*

[16] *"Who are you?"*

[17] *"My name is Nexhi, and I would like to speak with my daughter."*

My mother could hear Rita speaking to my father in the background. *Where is Angela?* she wondered, desperate for my voice, my breath on the line.

She thought I'd be the one coming to the phone; she heard my father's voice instead. He spoke without greeting her first; his manner hadn't changed a bit. Speaking in Albanian with agitation in his voice, he barked, "What's this about your being here in Switzerland?"

My mother was unfazed, as if all those months of longing had transformed into grace and composure. "I live here now," she said with pride.

"Are you not aware of the fact that I can hang up this phone to call the authorities and they'll have you back in Albania so fast your head will spin? You've been red-flagged, Nexhi," my father said. "Do you understand the severity of the measures I can take against you?"

Perhaps sustaining an uneasy limbo for so long ultimately has the opposite effect. My mother was steady and undaunted. My father was no threat. "Put my daughter on the line," she said. "Or I'll put my husband on the line."

My father laughed, issuing a dismissive chuckle to indicate that he didn't believe a word my mother said. As he continued his threats, my mother handed Arnold the receiver.

"Good afternoon, Eduard. Arnold Nussbaumer here." Arnold's commanding charm was absolutely undeniable. "I want you to know that what Nexhi has told you is true: we're married. Her wish isn't to intrude; her wish is to see her daughter. In fact, Nexhi and I will be in Basel this coming Sunday, and we'd like to stop by to see her on the way."

Upon hearing Arnold's words and observing his gentle demeanor, my mother was overcome once again with an awareness that, at long last, she'd finally found a spouse who understood what it means to love.

XVI

The Reunion

My eleventh birthday had come and gone. It was just Dad, Rita, and me sitting around a cake at the kitchen table. That had been at the beginning of spring. It was already fall, and I'd lost all hope of a reunion with my mother. I never stopped dreaming that all of a sudden one day she'd appear at the door or that I'd open my eyes one morning to find her standing over my bed, as if she'd just materialized beside me while I was asleep. I often pretended that she was near me and that I could reach out and touch her, but my life in Shkodër seemed a world away. The sights and sounds were beginning to fade. I even strained to hear Mom's voice. I *wished* to see her, but I no longer expected it.

And then one evening in October, as I was reading in bed, my father announced that we'd be meeting my mother for lunch. "What?" I shook my head as if to clear my ears, as if I hadn't heard him right. I couldn't believe it—and yet I absolutely could. All along I knew what kind of person my mother was, how deeply she loved me, and how she always kept her word. My father stood in the doorway watching me, waiting to see my reaction. I was so excited I could hardly breathe, but I just shrugged. My mother told me she'd be here, so of course she was here. I acted like there was really no reason to be surprised.

My father then issued the following instructions: "Angela, darling, you need to listen to me." His face got very serious as he took a step closer to me on the couch. "You cannot say that you want to live with your mother. Do you understand?"

I just sat there, listening and shrugging my shoulders slightly. "But why not?" I asked.

He then looked at me with a solemn expression that instilled an intense fear in my heart. His face looked more than serious; it looked ominous and grave. "Listen to me," he said. "Don't you dare tell your mother you want to live with her. Don't you tell her you want to live with anyone but me."

He got down on one knee at the side of my bed as he jabbed a finger into his own chest, pointing at himself. "I'm the only one you're to live with. I'm very serious about this. I will never allow anyone to take you away from me. Do you hear me?"

"But all along I thought I'd be living with Mom," I stammered, barely able to form my words.

"You don't want that," he said. "And you will not say that you want to live anywhere but here, because if you do, something bad will happen."

I was scared. I imagined my father either hurting himself or hurting Mom, and I never wanted to be the cause of such turmoil. I was also afraid to cause any conflict between my parents—even if that meant containing my emotions and pretending I didn't feel the way I did. I remembered how much I'd hated the way they'd fought with each other before they divorced. At just eleven years old, I had the weight of the world on my shoulders. Whatever I had to do to avoid being stuck in this situation again, whatever it took to have my mother back in my life—I would do it.

The night before we were to meet up at a restaurant, I could hardly sleep, wondering what it would be like to touch my mother and throw my arms around her again—at last! How I longed for my ally in life, my role model, my confidante, and my protector. These feelings didn't, in any way, negate my love for my father, but until I saw my mother, my feelings of deprivation and loss would remain relentless and profound.

My father drove Rita and me to a restaurant in Basel. When we arrived, my mother and a gentleman were standing together waiting at the entrance. I gasped.

I ran into my mother's arms and hugged her with every ounce of strength I had. I caressed her face and kissed her cheeks, and all the emotion I'd felt for months surged out of me all at once. "Oh, Mom! I love your skin. I've missed it so much! I love your face! Where have you been? I love you so much, Mami!"

Tears filled my eyes and hers, and we lingered there in a long embrace. I thought I might be dreaming again. *Can it be true? Is she really here?* I looked up at my mother as though she were a goddess—and to me, she was. She looked beautiful, as always, dressed impeccably and carrying the vibrant floral fragrance of her designer perfume. Her eyes sparkled with tears and with love and awe over how much I'd grown. It must've been a striking moment for a mother to see her little child after ten months apart.

She hadn't physically changed a bit, but I had. I was still a child, but of course I'd grown in the eleven months since I'd seen her. I was developing a feminine form, and my long, dark hair streamed in waves down my back. My chiseled features had begun to reveal a hint of impending womanhood. Inside, however, I was still all child. My dreams were simple reveries of being Mother's Angela again, safe in her embrace, hearing her call me by her tender nicknames: *my light, my heart.*

"You have no idea how much I've missed you!" We took turns, it seemed, saying this to each other.

Arnold stood quietly to the side, not wanting to intrude on our bonding time. He knew how important this moment was for both of us, and he maintained a pleasant, respectful distance, When my mother and I let go long enough for Arnold and me to be introduced to one another, I could see the kind-heartedness and compassion in his eyes and in his face.

Inside, we all took our seats at a round wooden table. The adults took care to be civil to one another. As Dad and Arnold shook hands, I could see my mother doing her best to avoid eye contact with both Rita and my father. The restaurant-bar was as ordinary as you could ever imagine. We sat uncomfortably around the expanse of white tablecloth, as if gravity had drawn us awkwardly into the same orbit.

Mom looked so natural and at peace sitting beside Arnold, and I'd grown used to seeing Rita and Dad side by side. For a moment, I looked back and forth between the couples and tried to imagine where I'd best fit in—but the answer was completely obvious to me. The only thing I wanted was to be with my mom.

As I looked at her, still overwhelmed by the fact that she was sitting right next to me—close enough to touch! I just wasn't ready to share with anyone else, so I leaned over to whisper in her ear, "Mom, please come to the restroom with me."

There was so much I wanted to say to her and could only imagine speaking to her in private.

We walked to the back of the restaurant, past the payphones and the waitresses stationed by the kitchen. We stood together just inside the bathroom door, the pair of us reflected in the mirror above the sink. "Are you okay, my light?" she asked.

I was afraid that if I tried to answer at all, I'd start to cry as soon as I opened my mouth. She stroked my hair and started to tell me about Arnold's home in Zürich. "You'll love it," she said. "You'll have your own room."

She assumed, as I had, that I'd be living with her and Arnold.

"I can't," I said. I couldn't look at her as I said this, so I tried speaking to her reflection in the mirror instead. "I want to stay with my father."

With a stunned expression on her face, Mom kneeled down to

look me in the eye. "What are you talking about, my love? Of course you want to live with me. What you're saying can't possibly be true."

"Yes, Mami, it's true," I said, feeling intense anguish rising within my chest. I'm not sure why it seemed so crucial not to anger my father, but I believed that if he got angry enough, he could hurt my mother or hurt himself. *I have to pretend*, I told myself. "I can see you every weekend, though, can't I?"

"Of course," she said. She gave me a curious look and took my hand. She has the smartest eyes of anyone I've ever known, and I was sure she knew I was hiding my feelings. "We'll talk about it more later."

With those words, she led me back to the table, where a heated conversation was in progress between my father and Arnold.

"As I was saying," Arnold said, leaning toward Dad to emphasize his point, "Nexhi wants Angela to move in with us."

"Impossible," said my father. "I have documents right here in my possession that give sole custody of Angela to me."

"I know for a fact that you don't have any such papers stipulating permanent custody," Arnold said solemnly. He had a certain calm authority; it was easy to believe he knew what he was talking about and that he'd never bother to speak anything but the truth.

"Nexhi, tell your husband that you've already given full custody of Angela to me," my father declared, pounding a fist on the table.

"You know that's nonsense, Eduard," said Mom. "The custody agreement that I gave you was binding only in Albania! I signed that document knowing that Angela—for her own safety!—had to leave Albania to live with you temporarily. Under the law of this country, that document isn't recognized as binding. And now that I live here, I won't grant you full custody under any circumstances—not now and not ever." Mom couldn't have been more definitive.

It was strange to see my parents yelling at one another in German. I suppose they refrained from speaking Albanian so their spouses could understand. I knew an undercurrent of anger flowed through the conversation, even if I didn't know all of the words they said.

"I just want my daughter to live with me, and there isn't any amount of money in this world that will change my mind." My father's face turned crimson with anger. "What do you want, Angela? Where do you want to live?"

I was sitting between my parents, and when both of them turned to me, I froze. I couldn't do anything but sit there and rub the bald spot on my head. It was hidden by the way I parted my hair, but it had become a habit to feel for it with my fingertips, as if I was compelled to check and see if it was still there.

"Just hold on!" Mom raised her hands as if to silence my father, but I think she was afraid I'd repeat in front of him what I'd just told her in the bathroom, so the person she most wanted to silence in that moment was actually me.

"I know that it will take some time to get Angela back," Mom said. "It's unfair to overwhelm her in a moment like this! For now, I'd be grateful if we could defer this conversation for another day."

"What are you scheming?" Dad asked her in Albanian, so as to leave Arnold out of the discussion.

"This lady here," my mother said, reverting to German and pointing to herself, much like my father had done at my bedside the other day. "This lady wants to visit her daughter every week until the custody issue is settled."

"But she'll be in school," my father countered.

"Don't worry," Arnold said. "I'll drive here every Friday and save you the trouble of traveling to Zürich. We'll pick up Angela in the afternoon, and she'll stay with us until Sunday evening, at which time I'll drive her back to Basel."

"But she has homework," Dad persisted.

"We'll see to it that her homework gets done. You don't have to worry," Arnold said, hoping to put an end to the matter. "We'll pick Angela up next Friday, then."

"If you don't agree," Mom interjected, "I'll see you in court."

Rita smirked and Dad rolled his eyes. He turned to me and asked in Albanian, "When did your mother learn to speak German so well?"

Naturally, I didn't know what to say. I just held on tightly to Mom's arm, treasuring every moment and the scent of her perfume.

At some point, the waitress brought our food. The only thing I remember is that no one but Arnold ate. My mother kept looking at me with a puzzled expression on her face, like she was trying to figure out what, exactly, had happened to me while she was gone.

When Mom and Arnold prepared to take their leave, I clung to her even more tightly. "I love you, I love you, I love you!" I repeatedly cried, as if it were my last chance to ever say it to her. My father looked frustrated, and I thought he might start to cry. Instead he turned his attention to my mother.

"Nexhi," he said in a gentler tone, "I should say how very sorry I was to hear about Muho."

My mother froze, and it suddenly seemed like the world stopped turning on its axis.

"Despite the immediate circumstances," he said, gesturing to the frustrated array of us gathered around the table, "I hope you'll accept my sincere condolences."

"What?" Mom's sparkling eyes had gone instantly flat, and the color drained from her face in a snap. "What are you talking about, Eduard?"

At that moment, Dad seemed to realize that my mother hadn't been informed of her father's death. He truly hadn't meant to be malicious, though it did seem cruel to mention the loss of her beloved parent just a moment after threatening that she was about to lose me.

Mom settled back in her seat, holding on to the edge of the table. She was pale as a ghost. I'd never seen her that way.

"I'm so sorry," Dad said sincerely. It looked as if my mother might faint. "I had no idea that you didn't know. It happened two months ago."

Mom couldn't understand why no one in her family had informed her of this tragic news, even though she regularly called home. In hindsight, she realized that Muho hadn't come to the phone in a while, and when she asked to speak with him, she was always told that he was out with friends. Knowing how much her father loved spending time around the neighborhood, my mother never suspected that anything was wrong.

"Why did no one tell me?" she asked looking at her hands as they lay helplessly in her lap. *This was supposed to be the happiest day*, she thought. *How on earth could everything go so wrong all at once?*

She struggled to hold back tears, feeling as though she were the victim of a conspiracy, with all parties intent on excluding her from the most important, life-changing information and—all at once—taking from her the people she loved most.

Finally, the floodgates opened. A few tears fell on the white table-cloth. She rubbed them into the fabric as she said, "Please excuse me." She got up and headed toward the back of the restaurant. As she walked away, I jumped up and followed along, never wanting to leave her side. She looked down and saw my tiny hand in hers. Intense happiness and grief commingled in the tears streaming from her eyes.

"Mami, please don't cry," I said.

How can I cry like this in front of my child? my mother thought. I felt guilty that she now carried yet another concern—that I might actually be leaving her in favor of my dad.

She quickly dried her tears as we approached the phone booth. Mom dialed her home number in Albania. Aunt Edi answered, and before she could say a word, Mom blurted, "How could you hide the truth from me? How dare you not tell me that Dad is dead?"

"Wait, sister, let me explain—"

"There's nothing to explain," my mother said. "This is outrageous!"

"Listen to me carefully, Nexhi. I couldn't tell you because I didn't want to jeopardize your future and your reunion with Angela. If you'd known, you would have rushed home to Shkodër, which could've blown your chance at citizenship in Switzerland, and that would mean that you'd lose Angela too."

My mother stood silent for a moment, breathing deeply, as if giving the information a chance to be absorbed into her brain. Edi was right. Had she known about her father, she would've rushed right home.

"How did you find out?" Edi asked.

"Eduard told me—just a few minutes ago." Mom still shook with agitation and grief.

"But we did send word to Arnold," Edi informed her.

"Oh," Mom sighed. "Now I understand." She'd noticed that Arnold had been even gentler and more attentive than usual. She'd assumed he was just happy about their wedding celebration, but now she realized he'd been trying his best to shield her from this inevitable pain.

Arnold thought it would be in Mom's best interest to wait until *after* our reunion to break the tragic news. He never imagined Muho's death being part of the conversation at the happy occasion she'd been anticipating for so long.

When Mom hung up, she took a moment to get hold of her emotions, gathering herself as always before forging on. I knew she was still upset, and I gave her hand a squeeze. "At least Grandma Dava is okay," I said. "Aren't you relieved to know your mother is still alive?"

Of course I didn't mean to dismiss her sorrow over Muho. I was only ten years old and trying to offer some comfort. I knew I'd said the wrong thing before we even got back to the table and I took my seat once again between her and my dad.

XVII

Thank God It's Friday

As soon as my mother and Arnold got to their car and drove away, she burst into tears again, but this time she was unrestrained. Showing vulnerability in the new relationship was difficult for her. She didn't want to display her emotions openly, but under the circumstances, she couldn't help herself. By the time they arrived home, Mom was in a state of emotional exhaustion. She hadn't spent as much time with me as she had hoped, and her grief over the loss of her father was too much to bear.

"I'm so sorry for your sadness, my love. But this is life, and we cannot reverse what happened. We're helpless," Arnold ventured, taking Mother in his arms. "You need to get out and clear your mind. Why don't I take you for a nice dinner this evening?"

"I can't even think about going out in my emotional state," Mom insisted.

"I understand how you feel. I was in the same frame of mind when my dear mother passed away—but I know you won't accomplish anything by remaining here in tears. You must try to distract your mind." Arnold continued to coax her.

Finally, after a lot of insistence on her husband's part, Mom agreed. At Arnold's suggestion, a friend came along to diffuse the sorrow and engage Mom in conversation. It worked! Mom spoke freely and passionately about her life in Albania, about the nostalgic feelings for home that pervaded her heart, and about Muho, who, as Mom later learned, had begged Edi to tell Mom the truth about his failing health. All he'd wanted was one more visit with Mom. Tears flowed in abundance as she spoke, but the conversation was cathartic and cleansed her heart and soul considerably.

In the following days, Mom busied herself with attending language classes and visiting Arnold at his office. Naturally, Muho never left her mind, and she had to constantly remind herself of the importance of moving forward in spite of her enormous loss—and she would see me on Friday, she reminded herself. Though life was so uncertain, she took great comfort in knowing that each Friday, she'd be seeing me.

Fridays quickly became her favorite day of the week—and, of course, it was my favorite too. My mother and Arnold would pick me up in Basel and take me to their home in Zürich. We spent hours of quality time together, shopping, taking long walks, and frequenting restaurants. I was on top of the world, just being able to reach out and embrace my mom again. She was no longer in my dreams, but a palpable reality, always there for me, loving me as much as she ever did. Switzerland was no longer a foreign country, and after so much longing, I finally felt whole inside.

My father was well aware of my attachment to Mom, but he insisted on getting his full custody anyway.

"You know, Eduard, Angela is old enough to decide where she wants to live. Let's settle the matter by asking her," Mom said one day.

She and Arnold were dropping me off in Basel one Sunday evening. We'd had a particularly fun weekend in Zürich, which gave Mom the confidence to venture the question to Dad with Rita standing right there. We were all gathered on the sidewalk in front of Dad's apartment. Mom and Arnold had helped me out of the car with my bag.

It was terribly strange to have Mom right there in front of the building where I'd spent so many months yearning for her.

I looked at her and I looked at my father as I thought about the way he'd made me pledge my loyalty to him. I don't know why I was so convinced that the consequences of my choices would be as dire as he made them seem, but I truly believed that if I went to live with my mother, he'd hurt her or himself.

"I want to live with Dad," I insisted. "How many times must I say it? I want to live here."

Mom looked at me seriously, as if studying me, knowing something wasn't right.

"What happened?" she asked me the following week. "Has everything been okay with you and Rita?"

"Everything has been fine," I told my mother. Just as I'd never once complained to my father about how unhappy I'd been, I had no intention of saying anything about it to my mother either. What would be the point? I didn't want to spark any tensions between my father and Rita, and I didn't want to give my parents any reason to fight with each other again.

I suppose I was trying to protect everyone—an impulse that surely reflects yet another genetic legacy. Never once had my mother complained to me about my father; never once had she criticized him in front of me in any way, not about any of his bad behavior, not about their divorce, not even about his role in our landing in Albania without him and without any money. Mom had protected me by silencing her complaints about my father, just as her sister Edi had protected my mother by silencing the news about Muho, just as I—at eleven years old—was protecting both of my parents by silencing my own feelings. I complained to no one.

Even though I was only eleven years old, I somehow understood that this was all just temporary. I'd keep my mouth shut, and the day I turned eighteen, I'd be able to stop keeping the peace. My life would be my own—and I'd be gone.

"You don't want to live here in Zürich with Arnold and me?" Mom asked, facing me directly, holding both of my hands in hers and looking directly into my eyes, as if she and I were about to dance.

I couldn't manage to speak, so I just shook my head. *No. Nuh-uh. No.*

But Mom knew me too well. My behavior wasn't sitting right with her, so she decided to hire a lawyer. She brought a friend along to the consultation in case she had trouble communicating in German. As it turned out, however, she had no trouble expressing her love for me or understanding the legalese.

The lawyer was brisk but direct. He said, "I must tell you that under such conditions, your chances of gaining custody aren't good. I know you contend that the girl isn't telling the truth, so what makes you think she'll change her testimony in court? There's nothing quite like a legal proceeding to escalate tension between the parents in a custody case, and as a result, you run the risk that your daughter's turmoil will only worsen. I strongly suggest that you wait a year or two. Perhaps your daughter will express a voluntary desire to live with you as she gets older."

Mom discussed the conversation with Arnold, and both agreed to wait until the right time to broach the subject of custody with Eduard again. Still, when Mom and I spent time together, she presented plenty of opportunities for me to change my mind. There were so many openings in our conversations where I could've easily said, "Okay, I've been lying all along. Please, please, Mom, let me live with you."

But I said nothing of the sort. Instead, I froze. I lived to spend time with my mother; all week long I looked forward to Fridays, but even though I desperately wanted to live with her, I never said a thing.

XVIII

The Ring of Truth

ONCE UPON A TIME, IN THE ALBANIAN CITY OF SHKODËR, THERE
LIVED A SEVEN-YEAR-OLD GIRL WHO WAS AWAKENED EACH MORNING
BY HER MOTHER'S GENTLE VOICE, KISSES, FEEL-GOOD STRETCHES,
AND MASSAGES. It's no exaggeration to say that she led a charmed life:
her universe was brimming with activities, friends, and, most of all, an
unshakable confidence in her mother's unconditional love.

One day the little girl decided to test that love. She asked to go
outside and play, secretly taking her mother's diamond ring with her
out to the streets. She was a girly-girl who loved shiny, glittery things,
and the ring, her mother's only valuable possession, had always captured
her interest. As the little girl spent the day playing and frolicking, she
lost the treasure. She looked up and down the streets until it was nearly
dark, when she finally returned home without saying a word about her
transgression. The little girl and her mother lived alone, so there was
only one person the mother could suspect.

"My heart," the mother began, addressing the little girl with
great affection, "where is my ring? Did you lose it?"

"No," said the girl.

"Listen," the mother said, her voice gentle and her face full of love. "I don't care if you took the ring or if you lost the ring, I just want you to tell me the truth. I promise I won't punish you no matter what—and I won't change my mind or go back on my word."

The mother loved the ring—such a cherished and valuable possession!—but the mother loved the little girl more. Material things didn't really matter to the mother; what counted most to her were honesty, integrity, and honor.

The little girl looked at her mother's kind face and her pretty blonde hair, which always caught sunlight and shined like a halo. "I did take it," the little girl confessed. "I took your ring and I lost it."

Tears welled up in the little girl's eyes and her heart filled with remorse as she looked into her mother's eyes.

"Thank you for telling the truth," the mother said. "As promised, I'm not angry and I'm not going to punish you. It's only a ring. Material things aren't important. Only the truth has meaning, my love. Please remember that."

...

This is a true story. My mother taught me to always tell the truth, so telling the truth is what I automatically do—except for the time my mother reappeared in my life and asked me where I wanted to live. On that occasion, I lied.

I lied the first time she asked, and I kept on lying about just that one thing.

Why didn't I tell her the truth? Why didn't I let her know that, more than anything, I wanted to be with her and only her? I don't really know the answer. Some nights, I cried even harder than I had when I didn't know if my mother would ever return. For years, I kept on with this lie, and all the while it kept tearing my heart to pieces.

XIX

Building Bridges
and
Shaping Destinies

MY MOTHER HAD BEEN IN SWITZERLAND FOR NEARLY A YEAR, AND SHE'D BEEN HOMESICK FOR A WHILE—A FEELING THAT WAS EXACERBATED BY THE NEWS THAT MUHO HAD DIED. The fact that Mom had finally secured her documentation meant she was free to see me without fear of being kicked out of the country, and it also meant that she was finally free to fly home. As Edi had mentioned that day on the phone, if Mom had flown to Albania when her father was still alive, she would've had to start her documentation from scratch. Now, at long last, she was free to come and go as she pleased.

She was wildly grateful for all that life in Switzerland had brought her, but she simply needed to see the land that she loved again. Shkodër was permanently etched in her heart. Arnold, on the other hand, was less than enthusiastic about making the trip. "I'd gladly go with you anywhere, my love—anywhere but Albania, that is," Arnold teased. "The whole country is still in a state of unrest and controlled by gangs. But I understand none of that impacts your desire to visit. You're used to the terrain, the people, and the atmosphere.

For you, it's home. The problem is that I don't want you—under any circumstances—to go back there alone."

And so Arnold reluctantly agreed to visit Albania along with my mother. But the fates seemed to smile upon his selfless concession: as soon as the trip was planned, issues at work made it impossible for him to leave town after all.

"Here's what we'll do," Arnold said. "I've arranged for my good friend Loni to go to Albania with you, so you don't have to cancel your trip and I can rest assured knowing you're not traveling alone."

Mom was satisfied with the arrangement. She preferred to have a traveling companion, and she quickly established a rapport with Loni, as she had with all of her husband's friends.

"You know, Nexhi, I'd love to meet an Albanian woman," Loni confessed as they made their plans.

"Oh, really?" Mom said, and she was immediately struck with the image of her cousin Diana, her uncle Preka's daughter. "I know just the girl for you!" Mom smiled and pulled a photo of Diana from her wallet. Although she recognized the age difference between them (Loni was forty-one; Diana was twenty-seven), they seemed like a good match.

Loni expressed the wish to meet her. "I'll set up a meeting then," Mom said in a decisive tone.

Within the next two weeks, they arranged the trip, including a meeting with Diana at Grandma Dava's house, with Diana's mother, Karmelina, coming along.

Upon landing at Nënë Tereza Airport in Albania, Mom said aloud, "This is the air that fills my lungs and melts my heart!" She was flooded with memories, and feelings of intense nostalgia permeated her entire being.

Once she got off the plane, she fell to her knees, touched the ground, and then kissed the palm of her hand. This soil had raised the girl who had come so far—and now she was home. A piece of her had never left, and she couldn't help but feel overwhelmed by her long-awaited return; she'd been gone eight long months already.

Loni looked on in amazement. He'd never seen such a display of emotion in his life. "Nexhi, pull yourself together!" he said. "What's wrong with you?"

Mother was unfazed. "Please stay here, Loni. I have to look for a law enforcement officer," she said.

"What? A policeman? Where are you going?" Loni asked in bewilderment.

"Just wait for me here. I'll explain everything," Mom said as she proceeded to the information desk to speak with the officer standing there on duty. "I'm looking for a particular officer who helped me this past February when I was traveling to Switzerland."

"What's his name?" the officer inquired.

"I don't know, but—" Mom paused for a moment, trying to remember the physical details of this person who—in just that one moment!—had helped her change her entire life. "He was blond and very handsome."

"There's only one officer who fits that description. I'll tell him that you're looking for him." The policeman left and returned with a colleague who was, in fact, the same policeman who'd been so kind to my mom.

"I understand that you're looking for me, ma'am. How can I be of assistance?" he inquired. It was clear that he didn't remember my mother.

"I realize that you don't remember me, but I've never forgotten you," she said. "This past February I left for Switzerland, and I couldn't afford the small tax required before boarding. I was desperate to leave, and you helped me out, and I never forgot your kindness."

"Oh, yes! Now I recall. You were crying. You so desperately wanted to see your daughter." The officer smiled fondly.

"As you must remember, you gave me the money for the boarding tax, and I promised to reimburse you." My mother looked at the officer with tears of gratitude in her eyes. "Well, I now have the chance to do so!"

Ten thousand leks was the equivalent of eight Swiss francs, but my mother presented the young man with fifty Swiss francs instead.

"No, no, madam," the officer said. "I can't accept your money."

"But you must! This amount simply can't compare to what you did for me that day. My entire life hinged on getting on that plane, and your act of goodwill made it possible."

The officer gratefully accepted the money and went on his way, but Mom's acts of restitution were not over. Upon her arrival in Shkodër, she searched for the taxi driver who had taken her to the airport without any expectation of payment. Once she found his address, she didn't hesitate to send him one hundred francs. These gestures meant so much to those trapped in the poverty of our war-torn nation, and coming through on her promises meant so much to my mom.

She was overjoyed to be home and to show Loni around. "I wasn't expecting it to be quite so beautiful here," he remarked.

Despite the lack of political stability and developed infrastructure, Albania was rich in natural beauty—lush landscapes populated with fruit trees, fields of vegetation, breathtaking valleys and rivers. Such beauty didn't escape Loni, who'd expected to see a country ravaged by conflict.

Diana's mother, Karmelina, joined my mother and Loni for a scenic drive through the city. Though she had no idea that my mother was planning to play matchmaker, Karmelina turned to Mom and remarked, "I hope that you're not intending to introduce my daughter to a suitor like Koçi."

Both laughed at the reference to a popular Albania comedy about a city slicker's courtship of a village girl. Like Koçi, Loni looked like a fish out of water, gazing all around him somewhat astonished as he took in a new, strange place.

Their destination was Dava Ibrahimi's house, an old structure in desperate need of renovation. All the while, Loni's eyes wandered and darted every which way, giving Grandma Dava the impression that he was conducting an inspection rather than just absorbing his new environment. Everything was so unfamiliar to him!

"Where did you find this character?" Grandma Dava asked in frustration. "Is he a visiting guest or an explorer on expedition?"

"Don't judge him, Auntie," Diana whispered. "The whole country is new to him. He's just curious."

Despite his awkwardness, Diana liked Loni, and the feeling was entirely mutual from the moment they met.

As Loni continued to survey the house, the rest of the family arrived, greeting him with kisses on both cheeks. "Is this just a standard Albanian greeting?" he asked Mom.

"Yes, it is," Mom replied, knowing there would be many other traditions to which Loni would have to accustom himself.

Loni recognized that the family was warm and kind, but their poverty was striking to him, which made him uncomfortable and, thereby, inclined to make jokes. He couldn't help but notice that Mom's sister Drita had been wearing the same sweater for three whole days. "I'm convinced that she hasn't changed clothes in all that time," he said, holding his nose. "She eats, sleeps, and wakes up in that sweater. I've been watching her."

Having escaped this poverty yet having grown up in it, my mother was torn between empathy and shame. "Drita, go and put on something else," she quietly advised her sister. "You're making a fool of yourself by wearing that sweater all the time."

"Why would you even mention such thing? Did Loni say something about it?" Drita asked, her face turning beet red.

"No, he said nothing," Mom insisted. "Nobody noticed but me."

Had my mother never lived in Switzerland, she probably wouldn't have noticed Drita's limited wardrobe, and she felt a little guilty that she was able to see her family through Loni's eyes.

Despite these cultural differences, Loni's introduction to Albania and to Diana became something of a whirlwind romance. Diana took him to see a variety of neighborhoods, stopping to visit relatives, eat at the best restaurants, and take in notable and historic sites. Loni felt quite at home in such a generous, open, and friendly atmosphere. Even the shopkeepers took kindly to him.

All the while, my mother assumed the role of translator—finding herself oddly responsible for conveying even the delicate discussion of Diana's chastity. In Albanian culture, "a good girl" held off on intimacy until she was married, and Grandma Dava wanted Loni to know that her niece was entirely pure.

"A virgin?" Loni stared wide-eyed at my mother as he tried to make sure he'd understood Dava's comment correctly. "At twenty-seven? How can this be?"

Mom smiled as she translated, knowing full well that Diana would've been disowned if anyone thought she wasn't a virgin. It was far more important in Albania for the family to believe in her purity—whether or not it was true.

Before Mom and Loni returned to Switzerland, he and Diana were already engaged. "I care for this girl very much, and I want to marry her as soon as possible," he told my mother.

This made Mom extravagantly happy, as if it were a testament to the possibility of merging two completely different worlds.

...

Within a year, as soon as they were able to obtain the required documentation, Diana and Loni were to be married in Albania. Due to the country's continued political and social tumult, Arnold was still reluctant about attending, but Loni assured him that everything was under control and that Arnold would have the time of his life. Arnold finally relented, and when he arrived in Albania for the wedding, he, too, was immediately awed by the country's pristine natural beauty.

Upon their arrival in Shkodër, Dava was standing on the apartment's balcony, waving with excitement. My mother was so proud and happy to introduce her new husband to the family. As she walked toward the building while looking up at her mother and waving excitedly, she failed to notice a broken sewer duct beneath her feet, and down she went, into the mire.

Everyone began to shout for help while Arnold stood there, in complete shock. "Nexhi, are you hurt?" he asked with deep concern.

"No, but look at me! I am a mess!" Mom replied, feeling ruffled and uncomfortable—and smelling awful.

"Oh! She mustn't let her Swiss husband see her in that state!" the old women neighbors remarked. In that respect, nothing had changed—appearances were everything to the older generations.

Everyone recognized that my mother had married a good man. The entire family greeted Arnold with love and respect, marveling at his good looks and graciousness. "The third time's a charm," said Aunt Edi, and everyone agreed. With his open heart and his unquenchable curiosity, Arnold fit right in, never judging the impoverished condition of the house, especially when compared with his life in Switzerland. He simply loved the people and all of the new sights around him.

"Please translate for me," he said to my mother. "I want everyone to know how I feel about this place. You know, my family wasn't always wealthy. We had difficult times, too."

Dava was profoundly moved by Arnold's demeanor and his response to the family. "You've made a wise choice in marrying this man," she declared proudly.

Her mother's expression of approval was more than Mom could have hoped to receive. "Thank you, Mother," she said. "Your words mean so much to me."

That evening, Mom and Arnold went out for a stroll on the city's promenade. Instantly, the commentary of onlookers rained down on the couple like confetti.

"What a handsome man!" one woman exclaimed.

"How did she catch him?" asked another.

"Has he actually married her?" a third woman wondered. "Maybe they're just lovers."

"She's twice divorced!" the first woman chimed in again. "How did she get him to marry her?"

Strangers may have puzzled over my mother's societal appeal, but the people who knew her weren't at all surprised. "Of course, he's extraordinarily handsome and refined," most of the neighbors agreed. "Nexhi wouldn't have married him otherwise."

Through all of the chatter, Mom just kept on walking with a content smile on her face, grateful for all that life had bestowed upon her.

A similar fate was about to embrace lovely Diana, who married Loni in a Catholic ceremony. Diana was an exquisite, radiant bride, brimming with joy, as were all who knew her. Soon, she would leave her abject living conditions—a tiny two-room apartment that could hardly accommodate her family—for a life of comfort in Switzerland.

A crowd gathered to cheer the couple as they made their way to the church. "Well done, Nexhi!" someone called out. "You've saved her life." Similar chants broke out among those gathered—much to Arnold's bewilderment.

"People seem to be calling your name, meine Liebe.[18] Why is that? What are they saying?" Arnold wanted to know.

Mom hardly knew what to say. The answer was too complicated and lengthy to explain. Prior to this moment, the idea that she would become a hometown hero for orchestrating her cousin's Cinderella story hadn't entered my mother's mind, but she was just starting to realize that her own assimilation had equipped her to serve as a bridge between two very different worlds. She could not yet put this feeling into words, so she just smiled at Arnold and shrugged her shoulders.

The wedding reception was held in the old city's museum near the Migjeni Theater, and it was unforgettable. Diana's family couldn't afford such a lavish gathering, but Loni had stepped up to make the magical part possible. It was 1998, and the country was still embroiled

---

[18] *My love*

in political strife and poverty, under the control of criminal elements. Knowing this, Mom's uncle Preka had hired armed guards to stand outside the reception hall throughout the celebration. Loni hadn't been told about the arrangement as Preka didn't want to alarm the foreign groom.

"What are they doing there?" Loni asked upon noticing the men wielding weapons in front of the museum. "Arnold, did you see those guys standing there with firearms?"

Arnold became anxious. He hated the mere mention of violence, let alone any display of it. His face grew pale and fearful. "What does this mean, Nexhi? Why are these armed men here?"

Mom put her arms around her husband. "Just calm down. Nothing will happen. They're here only to protect us."

"As long as you're sure it's okay. Can you tell me, without hesitation, that all is well here?"

"Of course." Mother smiled, and Arnold was finally able to relax. She was able to bridge the cultures in both directions, easing her Swiss compatriots into her old world while helping her Albanian family acclimate to her new one.

Together everyone enjoyed a lovely meal in the reception hall, while Loni's mother, a sweet woman of Dutch origin, distributed carnation bouquets among the guests. As thoughtful as this gesture was, the Albanian contingent couldn't help but look at each other with amusement: Why would the dear lady bring carnations all the way from Switzerland when they blossomed everywhere in Albania?

Well, that was simply the charm and beauty of an intercultural wedding.

When the wedding was over and the time came for my mother and Arnold to fly home, Mom felt a wave of understanding that Switzerland had, indeed, already become her *home*. But as she settled in for the holiday season in Zürich, something was gnawing at my mother.

Of course she felt a nostalgia for all that she'd left behind in Albania—her family, her students, and her teaching career—while she also felt haunted by the fact that the Albanian people were still suffering in poverty. As happy as she was in her new life, she couldn't help but feel a measure of guilt. There must be *something* she could do to help—in her own way—improve the lives of others in the process of living her own. *But*, she wondered, *what could it be?*

XX

A Means to an End

Just a few days into the new year, 1998, the answer to my mother's question arrived—in the form of a phone call from Helga, Mom's language instructor.

"I just read an article in the newspaper about a new program spearheaded by the Swiss Ministry of Education," said Helga. "And I immediately thought of you."

Helga explained that the ministry planned to assist Kosovar families fleeing the civil war in their country to seek asylum in Switzerland. All of these Albanian-speaking children and adults would require German-language instruction. "Since you've already established proficiency in German *and* your native tongue is Albanian," Helga continued, "I believe you'd be an ideal candidate for a teaching position. What do you think?"

Mom was excited—and amazed that an opportunity to serve as a bridge between cultures had presented itself so quickly! "Do you really think I'd be able to do it?"

"Of course," Helga replied emphatically. "These children speak Albanian, and you have vast experience as a teacher. A Swiss teacher will be on hand at all times, so you'll be able to translate for each other."

Mom was giddy with excitement, her heartbeat quickening.

Helga proceeded to give my mother the directorate's address. "Their announcement called for applications, but I don't think you should send anything in. I think you'd be better off going into the office and being interviewed in person. When the staff sees your dignified manner and your enthusiastic attitude—and when they can see for themselves just how well you speak German—I'm absolutely convinced that they'll be impressed with you."

Mom thanked Helga profusely and promised to keep her posted.

When Arnold arrived home that evening, he was excited about the opportunity, but he had his own strategic ideas on how Mom should go about securing the position.

"I definitely disagree about going to the office in person. I don't think you should do that," Arnold said. "I suggest that you write first to the Swiss Ministry of Education and make a formal request for an appointment."

Mom emphatically trusted Arnold's wisdom—after all, he knew enough about how the world worked to get Mom a visa and get her to Switzerland in the first place—but the position was in Helga's area of expertise. My mother wasn't sure whose advice to take, so she let the decision slide for a few days.

Then, when business hours resumed after the holidays, she headed out to the ministry without mentioning her destination to Arnold. "I'm going out, and I'll be back soon," she said.

Dressed in an elegant suit and coat (which didn't exactly fit in with Swiss custom, but was a classic Nexhi look nonetheless), Mom was greeted warmly by two women and a man at the Department of Education's information desk.

"I'm interested in the teaching position for Kosovar asylum-seekers," Mother explained in perfect German.

One of the women began looking for Mom's name on the list of applicants.

"I won't be on that list," my mother said, doing her best to rally her confidence. "But I'd like to meet with the project director. I believe my background uniquely qualifies me for the position."

"But, madam, the list of applicants includes teachers from every region in Kosovo, who have lived here in Switzerland for almost twenty years. Two to three times a week, most of them instruct children in Albanian to maintain their ties to their language and culture. What do you teach?" the clerk asked.

"Presently, I'm not working," Mom replied. "But I *am* a teacher."

"Madam, you don't work, and you didn't apply for the job. How long have you been in Switzerland?" the information-desk employee inquired.

"For ten months," Mom said proudly.

"Ten months?" The woman was astounded. "Your German is impeccable—but there's nothing I can do if you're not on the applicants' list."

"Please," my mother said, composing herself and gathering her confidence. "I really must speak with the director."

My mother has always been relentless in pursuing her goals.

Suddenly, a man emerged from a nearby desk where he'd been quietly working. "You wish to speak with the project director?" he asked. "If I may ask, what is your profession?"

"I'm a teacher," Mother repeated.

"And you've been here for only ten months?"

"Yes," my mother nodded. "That's correct."

"Please come with me." The man pointed toward a long hallway, and my mother followed him into a large office.

The gentleman sat at the desk and picked up the phone to call someone named Marcus. The call was taking place in a brisk Swiss-German, which was difficult for Mom to follow, but she managed to catch a word here and there. Her heart pounded in her chest like an urgent drumbeat. She wasn't sure what was about to happen, but she had the distinct feeling that it would be good.

After a few minutes, the gentleman at the desk handed her the telephone. "Hello, my name is Marcus Trüniger," said the voice on the other end of the line. "I'm the director of Sonderklasse E Plus. I understand that you're interested in teaching in our project."

"Hello, sir. My name is Nexhi Nussbaumer," Mom said. "And I'm an Albanian teacher living in Switzerland."

"Where did you say you were from?" Mr. Trüniger interjected before she could finish.

"I am from Albania, sir—from Shkodër, a historic northern city.

"And what do you do, madam?"

"I've been a teacher all my life," Mom said with pride.

"Oh, you are an Enver Hoxha[19] teacher!" he remarked.

Mom was stunned and frightened at the mention of the dictator's name. She was afraid she'd now be seen only as a communist. "Yes, sir," she said, almost inaudibly.

"I respect all teachers of the Communist regime!" Mr. Trüniger said, taking my mother by surprise. "How long did you teach in Albania?"

She breathed a deep sigh of relief. "For almost twenty years, sir."

"Let me tell you, Mrs. Nussbaumer: I visited your country under Communism, went to several schools, and attended various classes, and I was extremely impressed by the work of the teachers there."

"You should know, sir, that I'm not on your applicants' list," Mom interjected.

"So I've been told—but now, you're at the very top of it!"

Mr. Trüniger explained that his assistant would be faxing her a form to fill out. She left him with the number for the fax at Arnold's office, and she hurried there as quickly as she could.

Just as she began to breathlessly report to Arnold all that had just happened, the phone rang. It was Mr. Trüniger's secretary, calling to confirm his fax transmission of documents. She and Arnold hovered

[19] *The leader of Albania from 1944 to 1985*

over the fax machine with tremendous anticipation, as if sheets of liquid gold were about to pour forth. When the documents finally came through, Arnold helped Mom fill out all the details. Then, he looked at her tenderly, his eyes filled with pride, and said, "Now, my love, go home and wait for your answer. I promise to let you know as soon as I hear anything."

"How can I go home now?" she asked. "The decision will be coming in today, and I'll be a nervous wreck sitting alone at home, wondering whether I at least reached the interview stage."

As my mother already well knew, patience is, most definitely, a virtue. As she and Arnold waited together for that all-important fax, she couldn't help but think of the waiting period prior to her arrival in Switzerland, when she sat and stared at the phone for hours hoping that Arnold would call with good news about her visa.

She'd waited for months and months to see me, fearing that our reunion would never happen, fearing all that waiting would be in vain.

And there she was waiting again.

She tried to remind herself that waiting would never last forever—it was just a means to an end. Her life was already full of evidence that good things really do come to those who wait. She knew this lesson oh-so well—but still! The act of waiting is just so excruciating. It's maddening, really, enough to make you want to tear your hair out sometimes.

XXI

Passion Happens

My mother was, indeed, granted a first interview for a teaching position in the Swiss Ministry's Sonderklasse E+ program. Then the waiting began again, before she was notified that she'd been granted a second interview as well. Breathless and ecstatic, she shared the news with Helga and Arnold before quickly shifting into preparation mode.

My mother gathered all of the documentation that would speak to her teaching proficiency, including photos of her students thoroughly engaged as they sang, recited, and conversed in her class. She was known for her in-depth teaching methods and her dedication to her students, who generally loved her as a person and often became part of her life beyond the classroom.

When the big day arrived, the interviewer, Frau Linhart, reviewed Mom's documents. She was impressed and requested an impromptu presentation, so Mom proceeded to expound upon her passion for teaching, the circumstances that led to her arrival in Switzerland, her marriage, her family in Albania, and her desire to further pursue her profession.

"How did you learn about this project?" Frau Linhart asked. "We need only five teachers for as many classrooms."

"My language instructor, Helga Hilmer, saw an ad in the newspaper and she thought of me. She opened my horizons through German-language learning. I know that you and Mr. Marcus Trüniger can pave the way for my career." My mother smiled.

Frau Linhart was taken by Mom's charm and her expertise. "We'll be glad to have you on board, Mrs. Nussbaumer."

She got it! She got the job! Mom was filled with anticipation and joy. When she couldn't catch Arnold on the phone, she went straight to his office to share the news. "Can you believe it? I've been hired, and I start work on Monday."

"Can I believe it? I'm surprised," Arnold chuckled. "But then again, it's you we're speaking about. Congratulations, my love!"

My mother had to attend an admissions meeting that Friday. Dressed elegantly and with her bright, enthusiastic smile, she entered Schulhaus Riedtli as if it were the bridge to a new life—and it was. Never had my mother seen such a school before. The halls and classrooms were flooded with sunlight, and the students had amenities—much like in a hotel—including a huge pool and gym. The school, built in the 1800s, was a historical landmark, but since the building was frequently renovated, it looked almost new.

All of the Swiss teachers greeted her warmly, and she was happy to learn that she wasn't the only Albanian teacher in the school. Her friend Nexhati, whom she knew from the Albanian Language League, also worked there, which made Mom instantly feel at home. At the meeting, my mother was introduced to Karolina, the young woman who would serve as the Swiss language teacher in the classroom. Mom would be her assistant.

The school board expected Karolina to handle fifty percent of the class time, while my mother took on the other fifty percent—but Karolina, with a new baby at home, was overwhelmed at the prospect of this schedule. So, my mother ended up handling seventy-five percent of the class time to allow Karolina more time at home with her new baby.

"Mrs. Nussbaumer, are you able to cover for Karolina, in that case?" the principal inquired.

"Of course!" Mom declared. "In Albania, we're quite used to working full schedules."

Less than a year before, my mother had been a woman in a war-torn region, merely managing to exist as she longed for her daughter so far away in Switzerland. She'd never imagined her life coming together so quickly and with such grandeur. Classes hadn't even started and my mother already had a promotion.

...

Of course, sailing is never quite as smooth as you hope it will be. At some point between Friday's admissions meeting and the first day of school on Monday, my mother managed to lose her new classroom keys.

"Do you know what this means?" Arnold asked, horrified. "If you don't find them, the school will have to change all the locks, which will be extremely costly."

My mother was beside herself. "I can't believe this. How could I possibly get through the interview process, gain the trust of my colleagues and the school staff, and have it all taken away because I've gone and lost my keys?"

How could everything be going so well and then take such a bad turn? Arnold offered to accompany her to the school's Lost and Found. The man on duty handed my mother a box full of sets of keys. "Inspect each one, and let me know if you find yours," he said.

Mom thumbed through each set as though she were searching for hidden treasure. School hadn't even started yet; how could she admit to the principal that she'd already caused such a big problem?

This is a nightmare, she thought. *I'm suddenly living a nightmare.* But then, right there in the box, she finally spotted her keys. "Arnold, I found them!" she exclaimed. She kissed the keys before even thinking to kiss her husband.

Despite that moment of chaos, Mom entered the classroom with complete confidence. She was simply elated to be teaching again. Karolina, by contrast, was a new teacher who tended to provide far too many personal details to the students. My mother, on the other hand, understood the value of brevity and self-restraint, especially when speaking in front of a group of Kosovar students from conservative backgrounds. Karolina was grateful for Mom's expertise and stood close by as if hoping Mom's authority might be contagious.

"I'm from Shkodër, Albania," my mother said as she began introducing herself to the class. "I've been a teacher for almost twenty years now, and I love my work. I'm married with two children, and if you want to know about my hobbies, the truth is that my profession is my favorite pastime." She had long ago learned that it was best to refrain from further detail.

The students then took turns with their own introductions, excited to have an Albanian teacher. Over the course of the next days, weeks, and months, it became clear that they felt comfortable in my mother's presence, always behaving attentively and quietly. When Karolina took over, however, the children seemed to forget all protocol.

"Tell me," Karolina beseeched my mother. "How do you keep class structured and keep the students so well behaved?"

"You have to be their teacher, not their friend," Mom advised. "A teacher can only control her students by being serious and setting boundaries. You don't have to give them any personal information at all. They don't need to know how you spent the evening with your family! Naturally, you mustn't be mean or cross with them. Rather, you have to win their respect, not their friendship. Be polite, and when you explain the lesson, try to look all of them in the eyes. Let them know that they matter and that you won't neglect them. Be authoritative, but kind, allowing them to recognize that you serve as their bridge to the world of knowledge."

Karolina was so grateful for Mom's willingness to share all that she knew. "There's just more one thing that's bothering me, though," Karolina said. "The students keep chanting the word 'dordolec' in my direction. I didn't know what the word meant in Albanian, but when I looked it up, I discovered the definition to be 'scarecrow.' Why would they call me that?"

My mother sighed. Not only was she a good teacher, she was also a master at handling awkward conversations. She suggested that they go for lunch and talk things over.

"You must know that the reason for this name-calling has to do with your lack of authority," Mom explained as they ate their meal. "As I said before, the children are taking advantage of your familiarity with them, Karolina. You also have to wear better clothes that aren't as sporty looking. 'Scarecrow' refers to your clothes." Mom smiled, trying to be gentle and diplomatic. Karolina was a sweet, intelligent young woman, but her clothes were entirely inappropriate for a professional setting.

"What's wrong with my clothes?" the young teacher asked, bewildered.

"To be honest, they're old and wrinkled," Mom said. "You're the authority figure and should present yourself in a dignified man- ner—which is easy to address now that you're aware of it. Because none of this means that you aren't a good teacher. On the contrary, I admire your practical teaching methods. I'm just giving you my impressions of how you might appear in your students' eyes. I have much to learn from you," my mother assured Karolina. "My methods are theoretical, but we complement one another and make a great team, don't you think?"

"We absolutely do, Nexhi. Thank you again." Karolina warmly shook Mom's hand.

The next day, the well-meaning girl came to work in more elegant clothes and with a changed demeanor toward the students. She and my mother continued their mutually respectful, productive working relationship, while the children, in turn, benefitted from a more structured environment, and things proceeded well.

But my mother was hardly shocked when she learned that trouble was afoot. First, she received a call from Frau Linhart stating that Mom mustn't come to work until she had the required insurance documentation. "You're at risk of losing your job," she warned. Mom called in sick, spoke with Arnold, and within a week, the matter was settled. Crisis averted.

Mom was relieved to return to the classroom, but she'd grown so accustomed to facing setbacks, it was difficult to trust that nothing but smooth sailing could be on the horizon.

And then came the issue of her monthly salary. She received a check for an astonishing 7,400 francs—which was surely a mistake. There she was, in a foreign country for merely ten months, without a bank account, and employed as a teacher's assistant. "This can't be right," Arnold agreed.

To clarify the matter, she called Karolina.

"If I may ask, Karolina," Mom began gingerly, "what's your monthly salary?"

"Two thousand nine hundred francs. My check is considerably less than yours," Karolina said. "There may be an error, but you never know. You might want to ask Frau Linhart if there was a mistake."

Immediately, Mother dialed Frau Linhart's phone number.

"That figure is exactly correct—seven thousand four hundred francs—and you have Herr Trüniger to thank for that salary, Nexhi," she explained. "In calculating your salary, he took into account your twenty years' experience and the fact that you worked under the Communist regime. As you may know, he thinks very highly of educators trained under Communism."

"Oh, Frau Linhart, I cannot thank you enough. When my

husband saw that huge deposit in his account, he couldn't believe his eyes, and I couldn't explain what happened," Mom said.

"Your passion happened," said Frau Nussbaumer. "And passionate teaching should be rewarded if possible."

With that, Mom expressed her gratitude again, hung up, and burst into tears. She was overwhelmed—not due to the amount of her salary, but because her efforts and skills were so highly valued and because she was going to have to trust that having one good thing happen didn't guarantee that a bad one was coming.

Of course, her husband was incredibly proud. That evening, as he held her in his arms, Arnold remarked, "My dear wife, you have been in Switzerland for ten months, you learned German in eight, and you're already earning more than I do."

Indeed, good things come to those who wait—and sometimes they keep coming, one after another.

XXII

Daughter with a Destination

WHEN I WAS ELEVEN YEARS OLD, MY FATHER TOOK ME ON A TRIP TO NEW YORK CITY. Rita was there, of course, but Grandma Angelina came too, along with my dear uncles. Describing how I felt about that trip to New York makes me sound like any other girl who lands there starry-eyed and dazzled, from any ordinary town: I loved New York from the very second I arrived. It was electric and it felt like home, and I knew without a doubt that I'd be living there one day.

What separated me from my starry-eyed counterparts was that by the time I turned eleven, I'd already spent nearly an entire year with absolutely nothing to do but think about my future. Throughout all those months of isolation and longing for my mother, imagining what I'd do next was all I had to keep me going.

No school, no friends, just the radio calling out to me as I sat alone in that apartment—what else was there to think about? "So tell me what you want, what you really, really want," the Spice Girls sang to me from the radio all day.

At the beginning, it was easier to understand what I really *didn't* want: I didn't want to spend my life walking on eggshells around Rita or my father; I didn't want to spend my days longing but not having; I didn't want to pick where I lived strictly to please my mom or dad. I didn't want to live out the future that either of them had in mind for me.

I wanted to be a model. I wanted to live in New York City. I wanted to be eighteen and on my way. I wanted to get gone.

Yo, I'll tell you what I want, what I really, really want . . .

What I wanted was a life that was entirely my own.

All along, I kept reminding myself that living with my dad and Rita was just temporary. My life would begin the day I could finally leave.

As a frightened nine-year-old in Switzerland longing for my mother, I had no idea what would become of me. But by the time I was eleven and standing in Manhattan, my vision for my future was absolutely clear. I'd been to New York City in my mind a thousand times already. The subways felt familiar; the neighborhoods felt like home. I'd been carrying around the idea of living there for so long, and across so many thousands of miles, that I already knew exactly where I was going: I was going to New York, and I was going to be a model. You could take away my food, my friends, all of my creature comforts, but I learned early on that my ideas were my own. I didn't have to share them with anyone or hold out for approval. I learned at an early age that an idea was a bulletproof possession—the most powerful thing on earth. Nothing could shoot it down.

So I wasn't interested in telling my mom or dad about all the insidious things Rita would do to me, and I really wasn't interested in playing the part of a pawn in anyone's custody game. And so I entered a stage of adolescent rebellion, intent on going out whenever to do whatever I pleased. Mom and Arnold forbade such behavior, but it didn't matter. This made it easier to accept that I just visited on weekends. I didn't want to make waves or argue or get sucked into lots of drama. I wanted to keep my head down and plow forward until I turned eighteen and could be *gone.*

I was maturing at a rapid pace, and when I turned fourteen, Mom's attorney advised her that I was capable of deciding on my preferred living arrangement. Before the court, Mom insisted that I preferred to live with her.

"My mother doesn't lie," I said in agreement.

"I don't think that's such a good idea," said my father, asserting his control and his concern. "My beautiful daughter is fearless, unstoppable, and sometimes difficult to handle. She wants to do her own thing, go out at night, chase her dreams, and become a model. She needs strict parental guidance, and I'm the only person she listens to."

He wasn't lying either.

"She should remain in my custody," Dad insisted.

Mom and I both knew he had something of a point. I still lived for the time I spent with my mother on weekends, but she and I both understood that my father really was the only one who could keep me in line.

So Mom conceded and, truth be told, she was grateful that I was living under Dad's roof, subjected to his brand of discipline.

Throughout the week at school, I struggled to avoid the bullying that plagued me. The boys all loved to ridicule my accent, which bothered me more than I should have let it. I knew that none of them could've managed life in my shoes, dropping out of the sky from Albania and landing on another planet—one where you might spend a year locked in an apartment trying to learn German from an Italian dictionary.

My father taught me how to defend myself from the verbal and physical attacks, and as delicate and girly as I was, I managed to hold my own against the best of my adversaries. My dad taught me to fight back; he taught me not to take insults from anyone. My day-to-day experience definitely wasn't pleasant, but I learned to survive. I learned I had no choice but to compose myself and forge ahead, just like my mother.

Mom and Arnold never allowed me to go out alone, and whenever I was heading off to parties with friends, they'd warn me of the risk that drinks might be spiked with alcohol or drugs. Arnold couldn't have been kinder or more gracious with me, and I quickly recognized my step-father as a great humanitarian and one of the most amazing human beings I'd ever met, but they were always looking over my shoulder, making sure I did "the right thing," urging me to rely on their judgment rather than developing my own.

Though I'd spent so much time unwillingly isolated, like most teenagers, I began to escape to the quiet of my room. I already knew where I wanted to go and what I wanted to be, so I spent a lot of time imagining how I'd get there. The British singer Craig David dominated the soundtrack of my life at that time. He sang about everything I felt—wanting to "walk away from the troubles in my life to find a better day." And I found inspiration in believing that there would be better days ahead when I could walk away from Switzerland.

I'm going to New York City, and I will become a model, I told myself. My mother had already taught me many things, and chief among them was that you had to set your sights and keep on going. She had learned a language, acclimated to a culture, and become a bridge to students arriving in a new life as disoriented as she'd been. I'd learned the language too, and I'd set my sights—and just like Mom, I'd keep forging ahead.

XXIII

The Bridge to Integration

ONE DAY, IN THE MIDDLE OF HER FIRST TERM TEACHING IN SWIT-
ZERLAND, MOM RECEIVED A CALL FROM AN INSPECTOR AT THE
ZÜRICH EDUCATION OFFICE. He informed her that he would be
coming midweek to observe her class and that she had to prepare to
speak only in Albanian, without Karolina present.

My mother was baffled by this request. The inspector had been
to Schulhaus Riedtli now and then to conduct inspections, but his
request that she speak only in Albanian seemed extremely odd. Still,
she prepared as the inspector had instructed, and she arrived for his
visit with a grammar lesson for the children, which was mingled
with illustrations. Each student took turns at the blackboard, and
everyone was very animated and engaged.

"You're a wonderful teacher!" the inspector said immediately
after class.

"Thank you, Herr Inspektor, but we're all Albanian, from the
same culture. It's only natural that we interact well with each other."

"That's just what Herr Trüniger said, but I had to come see for myself. You see, we received a letter of complaint from fifty Kosovar individuals. They were emphatic that the languages in Kosovo and Albania are distinct and that the children don't understand your dialect. The complainants asserted that you have no place teaching here."

My mother's cheeks were burning, but she did her best to gather her composure. "Listen, Herr Inspektor. It would take a considerable amount of time to explain how the Albanian language in the two countries differs only in dialect, but I can do so if you wish."

"That's unnecessary," he said. "I'm fully aware of the differences between Gegë and Toskë, but after receiving the complaint, I thought it best to see your class in person."

"I speak the Gegë dialect since I am from Shkodër, a historic city in Northern Albania, but as you know, I must avoid all dialects when teaching and try to speak standard Albanian. I suggest that my students do the same, although we converse in Gegë. In any case," Mom said, "I assure you that we understand each other perfectly."

"I observed that, and my time was not at all wasted here. I can see that you're a born teacher, and it was a great pleasure to meet you," the inspector replied, shaking my mother's hand.

...

Two months later, a Swiss television channel requested permission to shoot a piece about bilingual classes at the school. Reporters would interview the teachers and film some of the lessons.

My mother could hardly contain her excitement, and on the designated day, she, Karolina, and the other teachers appeared for interviews in front of reporters and Mr. Trüniger, the head of the Bern Educational Department.

Mr. Trüniger was, of course, the man who'd hired my mother, though this was the first time they'd met in person. He was a man of about her age, short in stature, with long hair and a gracious manner.

"Is it true you've only been in Switzerland for a year now?" he asked.

"Yes," my mother answered modestly.

"Well, it's amazing how quickly you learned our language. I congratulate you," he said.

At that moment, a reporter interrupted the conversation. "Mrs. Nussbaumer, can you tell us how you feel about this project? What do you think of the Swiss government's initiative?"

"The program is a miracle for the kids!" my mother said enthusiastically. "All of them have emerged from a tragic war, impoverished, hungry, and barely able to survive. I call this project a miracle because there's nowhere else in the world where they could receive such support."

Over the next few days, these words became headline news. That very evening, she appeared on the main news channel. Her name appeared beneath her image: *Nexhmije Nussbaumer, Albanian teacher.*

Arnold marveled at my mother's overnight success, while all of Arnold's friends and relatives called to say that they'd seen her on the news. Seeing her name as it appeared on the screen, many of them were now moved to ask about its origin. She explained that her name wasn't actually Albanian, but Arabic, meaning *star.*

(I personally have always believed that my mom's name was no coincidence; she has always been—and remains—a shining light to everyone she knows.)

Later that week, Mom received a letter from Mr. Trüniger, congratulating her on her fine work and wishing her all the best her profession could offer.

Mom had found her niche in a foreign country, learning to speak and teach a language she'd hardly even heard just twelve months prior.

...

A year and a half later, when the war in Kosovo was over, most of the children returned to their country and the program closed. Mother was showered with gifts, postcards, farewell wishes, and love. Like all of the students, teachers, and families associated with the program, she was sad to see her class come to an end. She'd truly come to love everyone in Sonderklasse E+.

When she first became unemployed, my mother actively searched for new employment, even though she still retained 75 percent of her last salary. As she looked for work, she decided to gather the Kosovar children who'd managed to remain behind and she offered to continue teaching them for free.

Of course, the children and their families joyfully agreed. Within just two months' time, my mother put together a band of her musical students. The group was quickly invited to perform at children's parties in Zürich. Before long, she also became part of Perparimi's board of directors. As it was a nonprofit organization, Mother wasn't paid for her participation; she simply loved the work.

On one of Mr. Trüniger's visits to the organization's meeting venue, he asked if she would be interested in spearheading a project related to women.

"Of course, I would, sir," she said. "I taught German to recently arrived Kosovar women in Switzerland, and I believe that these women would be an ideal focus for me."

"What makes these women particularly interesting to you, Frau Nexhi?" Mr. Trüniger inquired.

"When I first arrived here, I was struck by the poor educational background of most of the Albanian Macedonian and Kosovar women I encountered. Many had barely completed elementary school; they'd been forced to quit due to the war. They couldn't speak German at all, even though they'd been in Switzerland for a decade or more. And they weren't literate in Albanian either. I felt for them, knowing firsthand how difficult it is to establish oneself without the native language."

Mr. Trüniger nodded and encouraged my mother to do some research on the educational system in Kosovo. Afterward, they would speak again.

Mom's research bore out her assumptions: Schools had closed during the war, and people had used basements as rudimentary classrooms. Even when conditions had somewhat improved, the education system continued to be subpar, especially in the distant villages.

"If it was difficult for me, as a well-educated woman and teacher, to learn German," she said to Arnold, "can you imagine how difficult it must be for women who are poor, uneducated, and sheltered from the world?"

How can I be of help? Mother wondered to herself.

After much reflection, Mom went to visit Mr. Trüniger in his office to propose a new women's program.

"A program for Albanian Macedonian and Kosovar women is essential," she said, taking a seat across from Mr. Trüniger. "Albanian Macedonian and Kosovar women have been subjugated not only by war—but also by their husbands. They've been kept in the home and isolated from the world. As a result, when they come to Switzerland, it's not just the language that's unfamiliar—it's everything. It's entirely new for them to participate in society."

"Go on," Mr. Trüniger nodded, urging Mom to continue.

"We need to establish German-language courses designed for these women," she said.

"But we already have many language centers. We have elementary, intermediate, and advanced courses all over the country, wherever Albanians and other foreigners reside," Mr. Trüniger interjected.

"That's true," Mom said. "But we need courses that are specific to these women—and we need *Albanian* instructors to teach them."

"We have our teachers, Nexhi, and they're very good at what they do. How can Albanian teachers improve the instructional coursework?"

"I realize that you have excellent teachers; I've studied with one, and she was so wonderful that she's now a dear friend. But I must confess that for an entire month, I had no idea what she was saying. I didn't know a word of German at the time, and I found learning extremely difficult. But it's not just the native language of the teacher," Mom continued. "We need to offer language classes that are relevant to these women. Then the classes will be *motivational* for them. These women can come to class feeling enthusiastic from day one, knowing that their Albanian teacher was once in their shoes."

Mr. Trüniger was frantically taking notes.

"I want to make all the lessons relevant to the new challenges these women face here. One woman told me that she was irate because the school wanted to send her child to a therapist. It was no small feat explaining to her that a speech therapist isn't employed to diagnose mental problems but to assist children in language proficiency and their ability to communicate. These classes must offer *more* than language; these women must learn about this culture and its institutions. They must learn how to actually *live* here."

Mr. Trüniger looked up from his notepad. He'd been scribbling on his notepad the entire time my mother spoke. "What level of education should the Albanian teacher have?"

"She should be an educator and be able to speak German," Mom said decisively.

"Like you?" he remarked.

"Perhaps, Mr. Trüniger, you believe I'm not ready for such a position yet, but—"

"I'm not saying that, Nexhi. What I'm saying is that I'm impressed by your courage and strength." He gave Mom a moment to absorb these words, as if he personally understood that the bravest and strongest among us hardly feel that way at all.

He continued, "But how can you help them in German? Although you converse remarkably well, it isn't your native tongue."

"I understand, but I can certainly help the women learn how to have simple conversations in standard German, how to address their children's teachers, how *not* to use the Swiss-German dialect, and how to interact in society. I can teach them not to be afraid of the speech therapist at their children's school."

Marcus resumed writing down everything Mom suggested.

"I'll base my instruction on my personal experiences," my mother said, and she began to itemize the seemingly simple things that make the life of an immigrant so impossibly hard: how to pay bus fare and get around, how to navigate the supermarkets, how to behave in various public places, the general etiquette of the nation. "All of that was new and mysterious to me when I first arrived in this country," my mother said. "All of it was different from home."

Mr. Trüniger smiled and excitedly drummed his fingers on his notepad. "I'm going to think this over very carefully and get back to you about putting together a proposal. Do you already have a name for the project in mind?"

Mom was unprepared for the question and thought for a moment. "This project will be a bridge to integration, assisting women in adapting to life in Switzerland, but as of now, I haven't come up with an exact name."

"What do you think of 'Integration and Support for Albanian Women in the Zürich Canton'?"

"That's a very appropriate name, Mr. Trüniger," my mother said, trying to contain her excitement. The mention of a name made the project seem like a real possibility.

"Call me Marcus," he said. He explained that my mother would be the one to deliver the proposal presentation, and if the project were approved, it would be a pilot project for a year. "Of course, you'll be the one to direct it, so if you succeed, it's all the more likely to be renewed."

My mother was so excited she could hardly keep herself from jumping up and down in glee. "One step at a time, Marcus," she said calmly instead. "One step at a time."

...

A few days later, Mom returned to Marcus Trüniger's office. This time he presented her with an official six-page document—one that was filled with terms and phrases she didn't understand. "Thank you for drawing up this presentation, Marcus, but there's a problem." My mother felt defeated, as if she'd hit the same sort of wall she hoped to help her students avoid. How could she help them if she couldn't make sense of a project she'd been obsessing over for days? "I don't understand this document. My vocabulary in German is fairly basic. How can I make a presentation when I can't comprehend what I'm saying?"

Marcus nodded and smiled, realizing that my mother's dilemma was precisely the kind of situation to which her students would relate. "Why don't you go home and take a little time with the document," Marcus suggested. "Translate it, and come back to my office when you're ready."

That night, Mother carefully combed through the document with her Albanian-German dictionary at her side. She was astonished to see what Marcus had composed. "Marcus," she said as she took a seat in his office again. "I must say that I was so surprised and impressed by the detail and passion that you brought to the proposal," she declared.

Marcus laughed. "That's all *your* passion, Nexhi. Those are *your* details. Don't you remember how frantically I was writing down everything you said? I simply took notes and set your ideas to paper in formal terms."

"Thank you so much for your help," Mom replied. She was beaming as she extended her hand. She sensed she had a true ally in Marcus Trüniger.

As soon as she left the office, Mom mailed the application to Bern. She was among several other applicants—and she was the only Albanian among them. They others were from Switzerland, Kosovo, or Macedonia. One of the Swiss women was married to a Albanian Macedonian and spoke Albanian quite well. She'd prepared a program designed to make the Kosovar women feel at home. The idea was to sit on rugs around the room, drinking Turkish coffee and chatting. This, of course, was the direct opposite of my mother's integrative, motivational, and practical curriculum.

The group of applicants was called together to share their ideas in a meeting. Taking Marcus's advice, Mom decided to emphasize the motivational component of her plan.

"What do you mean by 'motivational,' Mrs. Nussbaumer?" one of the other applicants interjected. "Why do you believe that Kosovar women need to be motivated?"

"I'm speaking about lonely, isolated housewives who are not integrated into society—those who are poor and uneducated," Mother explained.

"Poorly educated Kosovar women?" said another woman, raising her voice in offense. "You seem to be unfamiliar with the individuals we're hoping to serve."

"What about the language aspect of your program model?" another applicant asked. "Do you already have a German-language instructor for your project, Mrs. Nussbaumer?"

"I'll teach them myself," my mother answered.

The woman raised her eyebrows. "You?" she inquired sarcastically. "Do you know what you're saying? I suggest that you take language instruction yourself."

Why is it so impossible, Mom wondered, *to put forward an idea without so many feeling compelled to squash all your passion?*

Just then, Trëndelina, a Albanian Macedonian woman, intervened. "Let's stop this. We're here to introduce our projects, not to argue," she said. "Besides, the final decision will be made in Bern."

"This is unbelievable," one Kosovar woman railed, refusing to calm down. "Mrs. Nussbaumer has been in Switzerland for only two years, and she intends to teach German! It's completely unacceptable."

"We'll see about that," my mother said. As she left the room, she did her best to suppress her feelings of humiliation. She deeply believed in her project, and in her gut, she harbored the belief that she would prevail.

I can only imagine how the cruel jealousy and competition stung—especially since Mom's intention was only to serve as a bridge, helping each woman become empowered enough to thrive in this new country on her own. *If I can acclimate to Zürich, so can you!*

Just like the women she wanted to help, Mom knew what it was like to be isolated and alone, undermined by men, and facing an uncertain future in a foreign country without support or proper communication skills. She'd had to prove herself a thousand times over, and she'd managed to rise to each occasion with courage and determination. All she wanted was to help these women see that they could do the same.

In her role at Frauentisch (Ladies' Table), an Albanian women's group that met once a month under the guidance of a Swiss project manager, my mother spoke with gentle authority on the topics of education, family, and health issues. She recruited for the group by explaining that everything the woman learned would benefit the whole family in easing their integration into Swiss culture. An advocate of women's health, Mom equipped these women with the information and confidence to speak to doctors and learn how to care for their own bodies. Her talks made such an impact that many believed she was a doctor herself.

No matter what happened with her Kosovo project proposal, the success of her work with Frauentisch proved to my mother that she was on the right track.

Three months after the disturbing applicants' meeting, my mother received a substantial manila envelope containing the following letter:

Dear Mrs. Nussbaumer,

Thank you for submitting your dynamic project proposal. We believe your innovative ideas are likely to be effective in helping Kosovar and Albanian Macedonian women integrate into Swiss society, and we're proud to offer funding to bring this program to life, initially as a pilot project set to run for one year.

Mom was beside herself with joy. Almost immediately, she began receiving congratulatory emails and calls, one of which came from an elite Kosovar friend who sat on the selection committee.

Congratulations on your achievement, Nexhi! We need you to be as strong as I was told you were at the applicants' meeting. The whole committee loves the project, so rest assured you proved those doubters wrong! Keep it up, my brave friend! We need innovators like you!

Mom was deeply moved by the note, and she resolved to focus her attention on its validation rather than the naysayers.

...

As soon as the necessary funds for the project became available in the Perparimi organization's account, Mom began to consult with the board of directors to develop the details of the plan.

My mother was designated as the project's leader, and she enlisted Marcus and two others to come on board as her partners.

My mother's primary concern was how to recruit women. Someone was quick to suggest fliers, though Mom knew that people often threw them away before even taking the time to read what they said. Which brought up another part of the problem—many of their potential students couldn't read at all.

"I believe that speaking to people directly or over the radio will be far more effective," Mom said. "Word of mouth is simply the oldest and most efficient form of marketing there is."

Mom threw herself into this endeavor, approaching women and speaking to them candidly about the project's intentions and its potential impact on their lives.

Meanwhile, the majority of the board members remained more interested in disparaging my mother than in helping her recruit.

Some were skeptical about the project; some were judgmental of my mom. One woman approached her directly to state that my mother would be a negative influence on any and all of her students; after all, the woman said, what kind of role model was my mom, given that she was twice divorced?

It was maddening! While my mother was driven by the cause and working her hardest to effect change, with the exception of Marcus and a couple of others, she was surrounded by naysayers and gossips. Every battle was uphill.

The marketing strategy, the project's name, the selection of faculty—every step forward required multiple sessions of demoralizing debate. It was difficult to fathom why so many people wanted to weigh in on this project, though none of them seemed to care if anything actually got done.

One evening, one of the men on Perparimi's board approached her abruptly. "How did you ever get into Switzerland, and why are you even here?"

What? She was a grown woman trying to run a nonprofit educational program. Why on earth did that make her the target of every schoolyard bully who'd grown up to sit on the organization's board?

"Why am I here?" Mom replied. "I'm here to resolve the Kosovo issue."

Everyone around burst out laughing, and Mother briefly understood how bullying is contagious. It felt so much better to be the one laughing for a change, the tormentor rather than the tormented. Like most people, she'd been under the impression that educators and do-gooders were generally kind to a fault—ha! Her experience with Perparimi wasn't like that at all.

Even though the program was set to start in just ten days, Mom felt a mounting sense of hopelessness and futility. She couldn't sleep at night, and all of her enthusiasm had died.

"Arnold, I just don't know what to do. I can't stand it anymore." How on earth had her dream project become such a nightmare?

"Then you can quit, my love. Nothing is worth your physical and emotional health." My stepfather has always been the ultimate voice of reason. "I can see that you're not feeling well, and I'd hate to see your project done in by all these horrid, jealous egos. You don't need this."

It was a relief to hear this uttered aloud by Arnold. For weeks my mother had had the same thought circling around in her head. She immediately called Perparimi's vice president. "I regret to inform you, sir, that I must resign from my own project."

Mom suggested her own replacement—Sadíje, the teacher from Kosovo—and the vice president didn't even pretend to put up a fight. Apparently, Mom was the only Albanian woman participating in the project, and Perparimi was all too eager for Mom to throw in the towel and let Kosovo steer the boat.

She was relieved but heartbroken. The project had been her baby, and without it she felt directionless, abandoned, and alone.

XXIV

Powerfrau of Albania

THE VICE PRESIDENT OF THE PERPARIMI ORGANIZATION WASTED
NO TIME IN CALLING MARCUS TRÜNIGER. "I just spoke with Mrs.
Nussbaumer. She's bowing out of the project and has agreed to allow a
Kosovar teacher to replace her."

"That's absolutely out of the question!" Marcus was irate. He hung
up the phone and immediately called my mom. "You made it this far,
and now you want to quit?" he said before Mom even had a chance to
say hello. "I believed in you," he said with such crushing disappointment,
it nearly made Mom want to cry.

"I couldn't stand it anymore, Marcus. All that gossip and arro-
gance and arguing over every little thing. It's tearing me apart," my
mother explained.

"Perparimi is only a means to an end—to fund the project," Marcus said. "The program itself belongs to the Swiss government, which
entirely supports you."

Mom could picture the first time she and Marcus had discussed
the project. They'd both been so excited and optimistic. With Marcus,

every brainstorming session was productive and expansive, always adding energy to the project, while every discussion with the Perparimi people had been so maddening and small. Marcus himself wasn't the problem, and she hated to let him down. She sighed, letting all of the air in the world escape from her resolve.

"Have you forgotten that you're scheduled to speak on the radio tomorrow?" Marcus asked.

For a moment, she had indeed forgotten. It had taken them both an awful lot of work to get the broadcast arranged. All along my mother had been convinced that a radio broadcast would be the ideal way to reach the population of potential students. She would be addressing the audience live and in Albanian.

"I'll do it, Marcus," Mom said. "I'll stick with the project as long as you'll stick with it too."

...

The next day, Mom arrived at the radio station prepared to speak for five minutes about the launch of her project. The Perparimi board had advised her to speak in standard Albanian rather than in dialect, but when she stepped up to the microphone my mother let out a charming little laugh as she slipped into dialect. She always felt the most like herself when she spoke as she would in Shkodër, and if she was going to stick with the Perparimi project, she realized, the only way to get through was to be herself.

Besides, she knew that many Albanians were listening out there.

"Hello, my name is Nexhmije Ibrahimi Nussbaumer. I come from the beautiful Albanian city of Shkodër. I want to make an announcement. Soon, the Perparimi organization will launch a special project, called Integration and Support for Albanian Women in the Zürich Canton. Our courses are available to the Kosovar, Albanian Macedonian, and Albanian women whose studies were interrupted as their nations went to war.

"The goal of our project is to help them all learn German through integration classes, which will assist students with everyday matters, such as navigating the school system here in Switzerland and effectively handling family health issues."

Mom then proceeded to provide the address of the offices. Just as she finished her speech, the radio station's phones all began to ring.

"Hello, Shkodër!" A joyful male voice resounded through the studio. "I intend to send my wife to you. I'm so pleased that a woman from the great, historic city of Shkodër has come to Switzerland to help our wives. Shkodër's women represent the spirit of Albanian nobility!"

Mom's heart filled with joy and hope, and her initial optimism returned. That first caller was followed by many others, each one equally enthusiastic about participating in the project.

On the first day of class, Mom's excitement was at its height. She had only four students, but that didn't stop her from putting every ounce of energy into the lesson. She introduced herself, provided the origin of her married surname, and assured the students that they would be instructed in the basics of conversational German—their ticket to integrating into Swiss society.

As she spoke, Mother noticed that all four women were captivated. She continued to speak about the project's goal and the fact that it was funded by the Swiss government, which meant that the government itself wanted these women to succeed here! Last but not least, Mom explained her personal connection to the subject matter and that she'd been a teacher her entire life. "If I can adjust to life here," she said, "then, rest assured, you can too."

"Now, let's get to work!" she said. "Ich heiße Nexhi Nussbaumer—my name is, or *I am*, Nexhi Nussbaumer." She pressed a hand against her chest to signify the first-person pronoun *ich* (I).

"Du bist…," she said, pointing to each woman in the group to denote the second-person pronoun *du* (you). Standing near her whiteboard without relying on any notes, Mom proceeded to explain various expressions and phrases several times, writing them carefully on the board and translating them into Albanian.

At the end of class, she gave each of the students a sheet of paper printed with German words and phrases and their Albanian translations. Each included the student's name and country and the number of children she had.

"Miss Nexhi, excuse me." One of the women rose from her seat as soon as the lesson had ended. "Do you mean to tell me that when we declare who we are, where we come from, and how many children we have, we are making an introduction?"

"Exactly," my mother replied.

"I've been in Switzerland for ten years, and I haven't been able to introduce myself—until now. Now I've accomplished that goal in only two hours." The woman broke into a broad smile.

"You know, Miss Nexhi," another woman said, "I once had a problem while traveling by bus, and I couldn't even introduce myself to the ticket collector. I didn't have my ID card with me, and I couldn't understand what he was saying. Now I realize that he'd just been asking for my name all along."

Words cannot begin to describe the immense satisfaction my Mother felt in such moments. All of the negativity seemed to fade away, and at last she felt vindicated and valued. Her students weren't alone in feeling newly understood.

Word spread quickly, and within just two days Mom had five more students. To accommodate the newcomers, she went over the first lesson again. In the initial two weeks, she focused on warm-up exercises and simple conversations, alternating between German and Albanian to ensure that she wasn't leaving any of her students behind.

"It's essential to know the language wherever you live," Mom explained. "With command of the native language you can help your children attend school with confidence. As you learn the language, your children will too. They'll pick up new words as they hear you use them. They'll be able to speak to their teachers, to express their needs and desires, even if they start off with just a few simple words and phrases."

Mom taught the women how to converse with their husbands, which seemed to genuinely intrigue the devoted wives, who asked my mother to repeat those words several times. The group quickly became committed to their studies—and to their teacher, whom they viewed as a steadfast ally.

Within a few months, Mother was conducting three women's groups. One day, she received a phone call from a journalist who wanted to interview her about the project. The two arranged to meet for coffee and a chat at Perparimi's head office. When the two sat down to speak, Mom had a gut feeling that the interview would reveal her true objective to the public: her desire to commit to women from her region of the world and serve as a conduit through which they could find their way in an entirely different culture through camaraderie and language. My mother hadn't had such support when she'd arrived in Switzerland, which was why she was able to recognize the needs of her students—and why she felt it was so important to offer them light in the darkness.

The journalist sensed my mother's courage and poignantly captured her motivation.

...

The following morning, the interview was published in a popular German-language newspaper, on a page dedicated exclusively to my mother and the Integration and Support for Albanian Women in the Zürich Canton project. The headline read, "Ich wollte nur eines: Deutsch lernen." *I only wanted one thing: to learn German.*

> *This woman came to our country in order to dodge stray bullets on the streets of Albania—and the ones that ricocheted in through the windows, leaving her to protect herself in bed, her only shield a pillow.*

A teacher for almost twenty years, Mrs. Nussbaumer subscribes to the belief that learning should be fun—and she's grateful to the Swiss government for their support of this endeavor, giving her the opportunity to do something for her people. She wishes to emphasize that her language courses are free, as are her supplementary talks on health and cultural integration.

Still, Mrs. Nussbaumer aspires to do more. She hopes to obtain a substantial grant from our city hall. In addition to the government support her program receives, this would enable her to continue expanding the program and moving it forward.

Mrs. Nussbaumer is convinced that a word-of-mouth marketing strategy is the best way to reach the students who best stand to benefit from the program, and she looks forward to increasing the number of participants. Mrs. Nussbaumer explains that seven thousand Albanian women live in the Zürich canton—and only a few of them are integrated into Swiss society. The rest are isolated in their homes, cut off by their lack of language skills and limited by abruptly truncated studies, a situation so common to those living under the assault of war.

As for Mrs. Nussbaumer herself: Despite her own country's disruptive unrest, she was able to complete her education. She has worked in Switzerland since she first set foot here, devoting all of her energy to her job and her family. So far, she has worked as a teacher, a translator, and as a radio show guest. Even when she was briefly unemployed, she organized a children's club, never wasting idle time. If you ask her about her salary, she replies that she was never interested in that topic. All she wants now is for her project's success to expand to all Swiss cantons.

The article also featured her photo with a bold caption that read, "Powerfrau aus Albania, Nexhi Nussbaumer. She came, she saw, and she committed to her people."

Suffice it to say that, despite the rough start, Mom was so glad that she'd stuck with the project. It was impossible for her to imagine anything else that could be quite so gratifying.

XXV

True Colors

As my mother helped her classes of Kosovar and Albanian Macedonian women integrate into Swiss culture, I began to integrate more smoothly too. I suspect it became easier in some ways *because* I was sure I'd eventually be living in the US. Just as withstanding life with my stepmother had become manageable because I knew it was only temporary, so did withstanding high school! I had dear friends, but everyone knew I wasn't going to be in Basel forever.

In the meantime, my father's devotion—and his iron fist— helped keep me in line. His commanding presence and his good looks caught the attention of my friends, who liked to stop by our apartment in the mornings to pick me up for school.

"Why bother?" I asked. "I'll see you as soon as we get to school anyway."

"Yes," said one of them. "But unless we stop by here, we won't get to see your handsome dad!"

"Super cute!" said another.

And the third: "Hot stuff!"

The four of us would then head off to school sporting the dark sunglasses I'd suggested we wear, rain or shine. I was convinced that if we managed to stay on the cutting edge of all the trends, we'd appear to be a crew of VIPs.

I was also convinced that it was a good idea to bleach my brunette mane and go blonde instead. Obviously, there was no way to undertake this elaborate transformation in the bathroom at Dad and Rita's, so I decided to take care of it over the weekend while staying in Zürich with Arnold and Mom.

"How do you think I'd look as a blonde?" I'd ask my mother from time to time. I'd lift one of her long golden tendrils and twirl it loosely around my finger as we sat side by side on the couch. For the longest time, she'd protest whenever I mentioned changing my hair color, but as she became increasingly involved with her classes and students, it was harder to get her to engage the subject at all. But I'd made up my mind, so one Saturday, I went to the pharmacy, purchased over-the-counter bleach-blonde hair dye, and emerged from the bathroom to reveal my new image.

"Oh, my God!" Mom exclaimed. "What have you done?"

The look on her face was of pure shock; her mouth hung agape. Giddy and delighted, I spun around like a ballerina.

"Angela," she continued, "you know I never gave you permission to do this, and—"

"Do you think Dad will notice?" I teased, goading her.

"What do you think, Arnold?" she said. "Do you think Eduard will notice that Angela changed her hair color?"

Arnold laughed. "Unless he suddenly goes blind, I'm pretty sure he'll notice!"

I could see that my mother was trying to keep calm. In such moments, she was relieved that my father had assumed the role of rule-maker and enforcer.

As Arnold had predicted, Dad noticed the change—and he was

furious. "Go to the pharmacy right now, buy black dye, and change it back! That's enough!"

The law had spoken, and I had no choice but to comply.

My father was also adamantly opposed to the idea of my becoming a model. By the time I was sixteen, I realized that if I was going to pursue modeling, I was going to have to have a real photo shoot. Who was going to take me seriously with a portfolio full of selfies?

At first, my father didn't offer any explanation as to why he was so against the idea, but I knew enough to avoid broaching the subject with him at all. Modeling wasn't exactly what my mother had in mind for me, but at least I was able to talk about it with her. "I really, really want this," I said. This wasn't something I wanted the way I'd *really wanted* a toy as a child, or the way I *really wanted* to go to a party forbidden by my dad. This was different. The vision of myself as a model had become so vivid by this point that it felt as though the destiny was already mine; to tell me I wasn't allowed to do it was to take away a future I'd already built—even if, at this point, I'd only built it in my mind.

"You can't do this, Angela," said my mother. "Your father simply won't allow it."

I explained to my mother the importance of having a photo shoot. There was no way I could even try to realize my dream without a decent set of pictures. "What's the big deal anyway? What's so bad about having a professional take my picture?"

Mom shrugged. There really wasn't any harm in just having my picture taken, she agreed.

The shoot was fantastic. It was exhilarating to be part of the collaborative project that is creating a compelling photo. Holding the images in my hand, I felt as if I was holding a sort of receipt, a piece of evidence that I was on my way.

My father, on the other hand, was less than pleased. I'm not sure how my father found out about it, but he sat me down for a serious talk. "You can't do this," he said.

"Why not?" I insisted.

He gave lots of reasons: You have to do something safer. You have to do something more practical.

When it was clear that I wasn't buying his reasoning, he changed his tactic: "You can't pursue this because I can't travel with you. You know I have to work, and I can't be running off all the time to take you to pageants."

At this, I laughed. I didn't need him to take me anywhere. In just two more years, I'd be eighteen and I'd be able to go anywhere I wanted—whether or not he could come with me.

Once upon a time, there was a girl in Basel, Switzerland, who was exceptionally good at waiting. She'd once waited ten long months for her mother. The girl wasn't even sure where her mother was or whether she was alive or not, but she waited. She believed in her mother and knew she'd appear, even if the girl didn't know when.

And so, when the little girl began developing big girl dreams, it didn't matter when the people around her did their best to thwart these dreams, telling her that they'd never come true. The girl knew that when she turned eighteen, no one could tell her what she was or wasn't allowed to do; no one could demand that her life follow a particular path. True, as a sixteen-year-old living under her father's roof, she had no choice but to obey—but in just two years, the girl reminded herself, her life would be her own. All she had to do was wait, and the girl knew that waiting was no big deal. She was already very, very good at waiting.

XXVI

Beginning to See the Light

THE REASON MY MOTHER STARTED THE PROGRAM AT PERPARIMI WAS EXPRESSLY BECAUSE SHE RELATED TO THE EXPERIENCE OF THE NEWLY ARRIVED IMMIGRANT AND THE GREAT FRUSTRATION OF TRYING TO NAVIGATE A NEW CULTURE WITHOUT KNOWING THE LANGUAGE. This was the founding principle of the project. So Mom was shocked when the woman she'd hired to run the program's childcare center approached her to complain. "Nexhi, I don't know how you can tolerate these women. Some of them have been here for ten years already, and they still don't know the basics of the language. On the other hand, you and I," the woman said, looking intently at my mother, "we managed to learn German in less than a year!"

My mother has never had much patience for haughtiness. When she saw these women struggling, her first thought was, *We're in this together; what can I do to help?* It was difficult to understand how one woman could respond to another woman's struggle with nothing more than a deluded sense of superiority.

"Well," my mother replied, "these women haven't received the quality education you and I have, but they're smart and generous. They're good wives and mothers and—just like you and I—they only want the best for their children. They just need our help."

The woman rolled her eyes.

Mom was flabbergasted to realize that someone who was employed by the program could be so wholly oblivious to the needs of the people it served. "If she can't respect the women we teach, then she doesn't belong here and should be fired," Mom told Perparimi's board of directors.

Since the Powerfrau article had appeared in the newspaper, my mother's opinion had begun to hold significant weight, and the woman was dismissed from her job the next day.

The article had also impacted her neighbors, who now treated her with a new warmth. One day an elderly gentleman stopped her on the street in front of their apartment building. "Well done, Frau Nussbaumer," he congratulated her. "From the first day you moved into Mr. Arnold's apartment, I knew there was something special about you!"

On another occasion, as she raked fallen leaves in the building's yard, another resident of the building approached. "Frau Nussbaumer, I've so often seen you tidying up around here that I'd thought you were the cleaning lady! I had no idea that you were such an esteemed teacher. We need more people like you who are willing to take care of their neighbors and their surroundings."

Mom smiled. She felt a great satisfaction in making a meaningful contribution to her community and to society.

The recognition only motivated Mom to work harder.

All of the buzz generated by the newspaper article paled in comparison to the letter Mom received from Zürich's city hall.

Dear Mrs. Nussbaumer,

We wish to congratulate you on your initiative and offer our help in funding the project, Integration and Support for

Albanian Women in the Zürich Canton. We've approved a grant of 11,500 francs, and it would be our great pleasure to see your work in action.

...

The following week, a representative from City Hall came to observe my mother's classes. He was extremely impressed with her teaching methods. "It's truly our honor," he said, "to support your fine work."

"You did it!" Marcus exclaimed in celebration of the new wave of funding. "I knew you would! There's just no doubting that you're on the right track."

Working with the students continued to be a great pleasure, but working with the Perparimi board and some of the project staff they hired presented a steady stream of difficulties.

One of the women from Perparimi couldn't seem to stop criticizing the Powerfrau article, complaining that Mom had been too bold by speaking in the first person throughout the interview. "All of us contribute to this project. It is a collective effort," the woman insisted. "You should have been saying *we*, not *I*."

Soon after, the same woman hung a huge banner on the wall of the Perparimi office. It read, "Anmaßende Leute gehören nicht in unserer Gesellschaft." (Presumptuous people don't belong in our society.)

My mother read the sign aloud. It was the first time she'd ever encountered the word *presumptuous* in German. When she asked its meaning, everyone laughed.

"Presumptuous people are those who like to show off," said her ardent critic. "Those people tend to run after journalists for a newspaper story and take all the credit."

"Oh, do they?" Mother replied knowingly. "But how do they get those journalists to write stories about *them* in the first place? Do they propose projects, develop programming, hire employees, and recruit participants *only* in an effort to court the attention of journalists?"

"Some do," the woman chided.

My mother had no time for such pettiness. "Can you believe she accused me of this? Absurd!" my mother told me that weekend.

Much of the resentment she encountered was, no doubt, inextricably linked to the fact of her gender. The display of the characteristics that typically elevated men in business—assertiveness, competence, and confidence—reliably set up my mother for criticism.

Soon after the "presumptuous" incident, Mom ran into a Albanian Macedonian man from Perparimi, who heard about what had happened. "I know you're a strong, hardworking woman, and I don't think it's a bad thing to be arrogant from time to time. You need to be that way if you want to survive at work."

Soon after, the same man asked Mom if she would consider his wife, Diana, for an open teaching position. "She is a finance graduate, and I believe she'd be a perfect asset to your program," he said. "Diana is the instrument of peace in our home, and I assure you that she will bring that same harmonizing presence to your program. She's seven years your junior, but I have a feeling that you'll get along very well."

My mother was pleased to hear the man speak so glowingly about his wife, and as it turned out, everything the gentleman said about his wife was true. "You can begin working here right away, Diana," Mom said after their extensive interview.

And so began a lasting friendship.

...

Within a short period of time, the program expanded to forty women—much larger than Perparimi ever expected—or wanted. Her students displayed such fairness and generosity that she became enchanted with each one, inspired by their engagement in class discussions and their determination to build a better future for their families and themselves.

In her students' eyes, Mom was a lifesaver. Many would come to her, begging for a seat in her already over-enrolled classes. How could she refuse? Mom preferred to provide free lessons rather than turn anyone away.

Just as Diana's husband had predicted, the woman who was now my mother's best friend had become an invaluable asset to the project. Give the rapidity with which the classes were growing, Mom asked for a larger classroom, but there weren't funds or rooms available to accommodate this request.

"I'm going to request another grant," she decided. "I've made up my mind that until I receive the requested funds, I'm going to teach my students for free."

By now, everyone who knew my mother realized that her purpose was to give a face and a voice to the idea of justice. Though she was an advocate for human rights in general, above all, she was interested in women's empowerment. When men asked to enroll in her course, she turned them down, determined to maintain a focus specific to her female students' needs. Albanian men, she knew, were born with certain rights strictly because of their gender. By contrast, the women rarely felt entitled to anything at all—and these were the people she wanted her classes to serve.

At some point after her grant request to increase class size, Mom accompanied Diana and Trendelina (one of the children's caretakers) to pick up their salaries from Perparimi's head office. Much to their surprise, they were told that funds were low and salaries would be delayed for a month.

"That's strange," my mother observed. The Perparimi organization didn't issue the funds. The government was responsible for depositing payroll into Perparimi's account. Perparimi was responsible only for distributing checks to each employee.

Mom decided to wait for the next pay date rather than immediately pursuing the issue, but when the three women went to the office the following month, they were denied their salaries again. My mother was the only staff member with access to Perparimi's account, and when she logged in, she discovered that the money had been withdrawn.

"Where is our money?" Mom demanded of Mr. Vehbi, who was the executive director in charge of money management for the project.

"You'll get your salaries, Nexhi," Mr. Vehbi answered, explaining that the money would be transferred to each employee account in three days.

Three days later, the salaries still hadn't materialized, so my mother wrote an email to the project's board, copying Mr. Vehbi on the message.

Dear Colleagues,

I am writing to inform you that the project's account is empty. All employees (myself included) have been working for free for two months since we stopped getting paid. Mr. Vehbi promised to transfer the money, but our salaries have still not been paid. I hope that you will take efficient measures to rectify the situation and to prevent such an incident from happening again.

Respectfully yours,

Mrs. Nexhmije Ibrahimi Nussbaumer

Rather than feeling embarrassed by his negligence and attempting to rectify the situation, Mr. Vehbi responded to Mom's email by attacking her instead, ending his message by saying, "All of you know her, and you know that Nexhi is an arrogant woman driven to insult everyone inside the organization whenever she can."

Mom could feel her blood boiling. This was unbelievable. Beyond the issue of her own salary, she had hired employees and they simply were not getting paid. She quashed all impulses to defend herself and sent out a one-line message that indicted Mr. Vehbi without resorting to those words.

Dear Colleagues: Please be sure to check the project's account.

Thorough scrutiny of the account proved my mother correct, and Mr. Vehbi was called to an emergency meeting, during which he was severely criticized. This time, he was apologetic and promised to pay the staff in two weeks. But yet again, in two weeks, payroll failed to be issued, and my mother, Diana, and Trendelina continued to work gratis. This was the government's money, and it was specifically designated for payroll! Mr. Vehbi couldn't just decide to do with it what he pleased. Why wasn't Perparimi taking more significant action? Mom decided to appeal to Marcus for a solution.

"You already have a lot of support from the women in the program, don't you, Nexhi?" he asked.

"I do," she said. "In fact, I've been thinking of establishing a women's organization that's separate from Perparimi. Maybe we can inform the Bern office about the idea and have future project grants transferred into that organization's account instead."

"You're still under a one-year contract with the Swiss government to continue with the Perparimi project," Marcus said. "In the meantime, why don't you get started on starting up that women's organization, and I'll make sure Mr. Vehbi provides your salaries on time for the rest of the year. For the time being, let's not inform Bern."

Mom agreed and proceeded to plan and prepare for the establishment of a women's organization, which took shape quickly and was completed by the end of the school year. Mom took on the role of project manager, while Diana was elected president by a unanimous vote of the students. Mom was then elected vice president. Trendelina would be the organization's treasurer.

From that moment on, Mom severed all ties with Perparimi. She asked for Marcus's advice on where to locate the program and conduct its four existing classes. One of the community centers in Zürich was delighted to host the project. It provided Mom with three big rooms— one for language courses, one for integration classes, and one for the childcare necessary for her students.

Many people at Perparimi were skeptical about Mom having any success on her own, claiming that the center was too far away for any of the students to attend. Once again, they were wrong. All of her former students traveled to attend classes at the center; many even brought their friends along now that there was more space. Never had my mother imagined so many students! Her program was thriving, and she absolutely loved it.

Her impact on her students was undeniable. One in particular, Haxhire, arrived in Mom's classroom with so much difficulty communicating in her own language that she was unable to spell her own name. With a little help from Mom, however, she learned how to spell her own name and her husband's. Mom was remarkably patient and clear:

"Wie heißt Ihr Mann?" "Was ist Ihr Nahme?" "Was ist Ihr Nachnahme?" "Können Sie den Nahmen buchstabieren?"[20]

When Haxhire was able to answer each of those questions, she smiled triumphantly and exclaimed with great enthusiasm, "This project is my light!"

As if in a chorus, all the students sang in agreement, "Yes, this project is our light! It's our light! Mrs. Nexhi is our light!"

The word *light* resonated in my mother's heart, which felt as if it were about to burst. Tears flooded her eyes as she thought about the implications of what the word meant. *Light, light, light*, she repeated to herself.

The next day, she named the project The Light (Drita in Albanian). It was a perfect name—and she didn't even have to convince a committee to agree to it. She realized in that moment that she was finally at the wheel of her own project, in the driver's seat. No longer did she require a committee approval and support.

"Marcus, I am doing everything independently—I represent the project in meetings, I teach the students, I prepare all the required documents and reports, and I continue to train Diana in her role as

---

[20] *"What is your husband's name?" "What is your name?" "What is your surname?" "Can you spell the name?"*

president. Everything is going smoothly without the intervention of a funding committee," she explained.

"I can see that, and you'll have full authority and independence with this project from now on," Marcus replied.

With tremendous love and commitment, my mother began to run her organization. She applied to Bern to recognize the establishment of her organization, The Light. Her appeal was poignant and persuasive, drawing on examples from her students' everyday experiences as they adapted to life in Switzerland. In her proposal, she recounted a beautiful story about one of her students from Kosovo:

> *She brought her three-year-old son to the project's daycare while she attended language classes. One day, the little boy wanted to stay with his mom instead, so she asked permission to bring him with her into the classroom, and I agreed. One day, after school, his mother took him to the city center. "Just the two of us?" the boy asked her. "We're going to the city center alone?"*
>
> *"We are," said his mother with an enormous smile on her face. They had never been able to go anywhere unless his father was around. His mother hadn't known any German, and so she'd been helpless to navigate the shops and the buses and the strangers they encountered on the street.*
>
> *"Because of the language class?" the little boy asked, delighted as his mother nodded. "Then keep going there, Mom! Keep going, please!"*
>
> *Equipped with language, the mother could now access the larger world of Switzerland—and this, in turn, afforded access to her child, who marveled all day. "Now we can go out in the world even when Daddy is at work."*

In the photos that Mom included with her presentation, one in particular has always stood out to me. It was of a woman in the classroom listening attentively to my mother while breastfeeding her child.

My mother's proposal to Bern could have melted the coldest heart. With one look at the testimonials, the skepticism of even the most adamant naysayer would vanish into silent awe, like a faint echo in a canyon. The application made it clear that there was no doubting her passion or her impact. Now all she had to do was wait for an answer from Bern.

XXVII

Making the Cut

NOT ONLY WAS MY MOTHER'S PROPOSAL APPROVED BY THE SWISS EDUCATION DEPARTMENT, BUT AFTER JUST ONE YEAR OF OPERATING HER WOMEN'S ORGANIZATION, THE SWISS GOVERNMENT NOMINATED THE LIGHT FOR A UNESCO PRIZE.

Founded in the wake of the Second World War, the United Nations Educational, Scientific and Cultural Organization is dedicated to celebrating cultural heritage while equipping all human beings with the education and tools to participate as global citizens.

A special ceremony was to be held in Bern and broadcast on public television, and the prize would be awarded to the initiative that best reflected the organization's goals. There was no doubt that my mother's project was right on target. Equipping Kosovar refugees with the language skills and the cultural awareness necessary to participate in society was certainly relevant to UNESCO's mission to facilitate the sharing of knowledge in order to foster "intellectual and moral solidarity,"[21] but nobody actually thought

---

[21] *https://en.unesco.org/about-us/introducing-unesco*

my mother would win—nobody except Arnold, who was quick to suggest to my mother that she prepare an acceptance speech.

My mother laughed. "It's lovely to be nominated, Arnold, but I'd be a fool if I traveled to Bern expecting to win."

"I don't know about that," Arnold said. Since my mother had moved to Switzerland, everything she touched seemed to turn to gold. No matter how discouraged my mother got, again and again her horizons kept expanding. Arnold had already witnessed it too many times to count. He wouldn't be able to attend the ceremony with her, but he was giddy in anticipation of it.

"I'm so proud of you!" he exclaimed, his pride lighting up his eyes. He has never been one to hold back his emotions or restrain himself from giving compliments. In this way he has always been a true humanitarian himself.

"Don't set yourself up for disappointment," Mom said, always a little self-conscious in the spotlight. "The Light is just one of several initiatives to be nominated."

"It doesn't matter if you win the prize," Arnold said. "The nomination alone means you've been recognized for working in service of the collective good. But I still think you ought to prepare a little something to say, just in case. What if you win and have to stand there speechless—because you showed up speechless?"

It wasn't quite a speech, but before the event, my mother did write down some of her thoughts. Reflecting on the development of the project actually turned out to be an enjoyable exercise. After all, The Light was the culmination of her life's effort to date—a completely natural next step on the path forged by her own experiences and interests. She'd always been committed to the empowerment of women, and her arrival in Zürich gave her a new understanding of how essential it was to participate and communicate, to feel comfortable engaging in human interaction.

Armed with her brief notes in hand, and dressed in some of her best clothes, Mom picked up Diana and Trendelina and drove them to Bern, about an hour away.

The ceremony was taking place in a large conference hall equipped to hold seven hundred people. The chairs were arranged in crisp rows facing the stage, which was punctuated with a solitary podium. My mother hadn't been sure of what to expect of the crowd, but in her white blazer and black pants, she fit in perfectly with the humanitarians and academics already milling around the space when she walked in with her colleagues. The volume of chatter was almost dizzying, as hundreds of conversations filled the expanse of the room.

One of the foremost television anchors in the country hosted the event. He was tall and handsome, and the combination of his stature and his celebrity made him a captivating figure. When he stepped to the podium, the din ceased immediately and the audience settled in. There was something particularly soothing in hearing this trusted and familiar television voice describe the people and the projects up for consideration this year.

While my mother immediately felt honored by the nomination as soon as it arrived, it was only once the proceedings began that a profound sense of satisfaction rose up her chest, urging her to sit up straighter and taller in her seat. Until the host began describing the projects and the people under consideration this year, my mother hadn't had a chance to consider what it meant to be associated with such a group.

She reached for Diana's hand, giddy with a new excitement inspired less by the prospect of winning than by the mere fact of being in that room.

The host described an incredible array projects designed to cultivate literacy, social justice, and freedom of expression. It was heartening to realize the remarkable scope of the work being done right there in Switzerland, and it was exhilarating to be sitting among the people dedicated to such work.

Though my mother, Diana, and Trendelina were all sitting on the edge of their seats, my mother was so engrossed in the event and in the spirit of the organization that she'd practically forgotten that she was in the running for a prize, so it caught her off guard when she heard the host call out her name.

"And the UNESCO humanitarian prize goes to Nexhi Nussbaumer and her project, The Light!"

Thunderous applause shook the room. Trendelina gasped, and Diana pressed her hands up to her mouth as if to suppress a scream. My mother, however, sat frozen in her seat, as if caught in a moment of animated suspension, still waiting for a name to be called—any name—unable to absorb that hers had already been announced, unable to fathom that the award was hers to claim.

"Get up, get up!" Diana swatted at my mother's arm.

"Nexhi, it's you!" said Trendelina. "Get up there. Go, go!"

Tears filled Mom's eyes as she finally rose from her chair and headed to the stage. She laughed as she stepped up to the podium, feeling delighted and ridiculous beside the giant TV host.

"Congratulations, Mrs. Nussbaumer! We'd love to hear you say a few words about The Light. It's so much more than women gathering to learn our language and chit-chatting over coffee."

"Yes," said my mother. "It *is* more than that. For these women, it's a lifeline."

Even as Arnold had voiced the possibility that my mother would win, she hadn't actually believed him, even as she wrote her speech.

Her speech! Where was it? She patted her pockets, extracted the piece of paper, and stepped to the microphone as the TV host adjusted it to my mother's height.

"Thank you," Mom said, speechless even with her speech in hand. "What I'd like to do is share just a brief anecdote with you.

"First of all, I should explain that this is our second year in operation, and just before classes started, one of my students from last year visited with her three sisters-in-law, who all wanted to study with us. All three classes had already filled, each with twenty women. Regretfully, I had to decline. 'I'm sorry,' I said. 'Please come back next year.'

"One of the sisters-in-law was simply devastated. '*Bitte*, ich will Deutsch lernen,'[22] she pleaded.

"I was moved by her words, and I asked why learning German was so important to her.

"She said, 'I want to learn German so that I can speak to my children's teachers and to my own doctor. I want to learn everything that my sister-in-law has learned, and most of all, I want to learn the language so that I will be able to go out in the world on my own.'"

My mother then pointed to herself and spoke from the heart. "When *I* came to this country, my only desire was to learn German—to be free. Without the language, I was trapped. Unable to communicate, I wasn't even myself. I learned the language, and it means everything to me to help other displaced women accomplish this too."

Mom spoke with so much conviction and passion that the entire room burst into applause. I can only wonder how many people she must have reached as they watched on TV at home.

"What about Albanian men?" the host asked when the applause quieted down. "What do they think about all of this?"

"Most of them are grateful for the project," Mom explained. "They want the best for their wives—and from them. Most realize that when a woman learns the language it serves the entire family."

A representative from UNESCO then approached the podium. He presented my mother with a certificate and an envelope containing the prize money. He then pinned a glorious corsage to Mom's blazer to mark her as a winner to benefit the press and the other nominees who, immediately after the ceremony, rushed to flood her with questions and congratulations.

The official photographer snapped pictures as the UNESCO representative presented my mother with the reward. They held the pose for the camera, reenacted it, smiled at one another, and sustained a handshake for so long it was as if the moment would last forever—and in many ways, it has.

---

[22] *"Please, I want to learn German."*

My mother's work has a legacy that will carry on for generations, and in the photographs of the event, her face is bright with an
unforgettable joy, reflecting the light from her white jacket and the
enormous love that filled the room.

Bridge to the Future

I WAS SIXTEEN YEARS OLD THAT YEAR, AND I SPENT THE HOLIDAYS IN NEW YORK CITY, JUST AS I'D DONE EVERY YEAR SINCE GRAND-MA ANGELINA HAD MOVED THERE WHEN I WAS ELEVEN. I brought pictures of the UNESCO ceremony to share with Angelina. Rita and my father had no interest in any celebration of my mother, but Grandma Angelina wept.

"Your mother has come so far," Angelina said. And, once again, she told me the story about the time shortly after I was born that she and my mother sat down for an ouzo nightcap and a chat. Afterward, Mom nursed me one more time before going to bed.

The next morning, my mother was thrown into a crisis when she couldn't wake me. "Angelina!" she called to me. "Angelina, come quick!"

"Your mother was beside herself!" Angelina told me (again). "And do you know what I said?"

"You said I was drunk off the ouzo," I replied.

"Exactly!" Angelina laughed and laughed.

Like any typical teenager, I rolled my eyes at hearing the same stories again and again, but the truth is that I loved it. After all those months of longing for my mother, I'd never tire of hearing about her devotion to me. Besides, I could relate to Angelina: I'd told myself the same stories over and over again for months when my mother was far from me. Angelina was far from all of us once she moved to New York. She could repeat those stories as often as she needed to around me. I'd never tire of listening.

And I'd never tire of Rita's annoyance every. time Grandma Angelina told stories about our family before Rita was in it.

And I'd never tire of Angelina being right there in New York, a bridge to my future.

A Cross to Bear

WHILE I WAS IN NEW YORK, MY MOTHER SPENT CHRISTMAS WITH ARNOLD AND THEN TOOK OFF FOR SHKODËR TO CELEBRATE THE NEW YEAR. Due to the Communist regime's denunciation of religion, there wasn't much Christmas to be had in Albania, but New Year's Eve and New Year's Day there were all about merriment and celebration.

For my mother, such unfettered joy often had something to do with baklava. She could never get enough of the sweet pastry stuffed with nuts and held together with honey. She was notorious for sneaking "just one more piece," and I can't count how many times I've had to alert her to a tiny bit of flakey phyllo dough stuck to her lip.

Back at home in Albania that year, she settled in with family, and the baklava binge began, as usual, but this time, she became sick to her stomach and was suddenly overwhelmed with severe abdominal cramps.

Of course, this gave Grandma Dava a chance to mother my mom again. "Here, take these hot compresses and place them on your belly," Dava said. It was obvious that my mother was in significant pain, but everyone assumed she'd just picked up a stomach virus or something on the plane.

"I don't need these, Mom," my mother said, throwing the compresses aside. "But I'm very thirsty. What I really need is water."

"Here you go," Dava said as she presented my mother with a glass. "Drink slowly."

She stood over her daughter with deep concern in her eyes.

My mother gratefully accepted the glass, but she didn't feel that all the concern and water in the world would be likely to help. She spent the night in terrible pain, with her stomach cramps steadily increasing with every passing minute.

The next morning, New Year's Day, Mom called the doctor, who suggested that she go to the hospital immediately. She really had no choice but to follow the doctor's orders; the pain kept increasing. Even when it was impossible to imagine it getting any worse, the paid would escalate. At the hospital, she tried to describe her symptoms, but the excruciating pain made it difficult to breathe.

"Mrs. Nussbaumer, you have gallstones," the doctor reported after completing his examination. "And they'll have to be surgically removed."

Mom hesitated for a moment. Perhaps she'd just gotten used to the first-world facilities in Switzerland, but this hospital seemed particularly cold. "I'm a little afraid to have the surgery here," she whispered to her mother, who was standing at her side. The only hospitals Dava had ever seen were in Albania, so my mother found it somewhat difficult to describe what she meant.

But Arnold would understand. "I really don't want to have surgery—and I really don't want to have it here," she confessed. "But I truly am in terrible pain."

"Have the surgery here in Switzerland, my love," Arnold urged her. "Let's get you back to Zürich, and we'll take care of you here."

Mother agreed. She flew straight back to Zürich and checked into a hospital. Back in Shkodër, she'd assumed it was the old-world trappings of the hospital that scared her, but even now, in a first-world facility with Arnold by her side, she wasn't really any less terrified. In retrospect, I wonder if her bad feeling was prescient. She was terrified that she wouldn't wake up after the general anesthesia. She cried for hours, even as the doctors wheeled her into the operating room, reassuring her repeatedly that her fear represented only the most remote of possibilities.

Though I was still in New York and had no idea that any of this was going on, there were loved ones spread across two nations who were keeping vigil for my mother—Arnold and his extended family and friends in Switzerland and Dava, my aunts, and everyone they knew back in Shkodër. Everyone praying for her said the same thing: "She'll be okay. Don't worry. She's going to be okay." Hoping for the best, they reassured each other that the Powerfrau would come out of this strong and renewed.

When my mother opened her eyes, it briefly seemed that all the prayers had been answered and all the wishes had come true—but Mom's surgical wound kept bleeding and the enormous incision was issuing its own riot of pain. As she lay in her bed, writhing in agony, she thought she might be dying, a thought that seemed to be confirmed when the team of solemn-faced doctors entered the room.

"Is there a problem?" Arnold asked.

The head physician exhaled in a manner that conveyed absolute defeat.

So much for fearing a third-world hospital! Right there in Zürich a surgeon admitted to my mother that he'd inadvertently cut her bile duct during the procedure.

"Mrs. Nussbaumer," he said, "nothing like this has ever happened before in my entire career as a surgeon."

"This is extremely rare," offered another doctor on the team, as if to suggest that the freak nature of the incident somehow made the situation better.

The situation was very serious, they explained. They'd have to operate again in order to reconstruct the severed duct.

Understandably, Mom went into a state of shock and despair, shaking uncontrollably and crying out, "Oh, no! Oh, no!"

Neither my mother nor Arnold was aware at the time that patients rarely survived such procedures. Her life was in peril, but the same physician who'd just botched the surgery promised Mom that she'd be in good hands.

"Fortunately," he said, "one of the best implant surgeons in the world is here at the hospital, and he's already been scheduled to handle your case."

My mother couldn't bring herself to speak, so she looked to Arnold for comfort. "Aren't we lucky, Nexhi! Forget the fact that the first surgery was botched; just think about how fortunate we are to have the perfect specialist on hand to go back in and clean things up!"

"That, in itself, is a miracle," my mother said.

...

Adding insult to injury (literally), the miracle surgeon was delayed. It had been difficult enough to accept the idea of a second surgery, but now she had to wait for it—for an entire week.

She spent those seven impossibly long days wondering which might do her in: the relentless searing pain or the do-over surgery. *Will I make it?* she asked herself all week long. *Will I make it? Will I make it?* It must have been torture.

When the time finally came for her to be wheeled back into the operating room, my mother was visibly shaking from head to toe. She remembered the doctor lifting the mask to her face—and then nothing. Such a strange paradise to fall away so completely, as if one doesn't care at all if he or she ever wakes up.

My mother did wake up, though it took a while. Long enough to scare Arnold and the doctors alike. When she slowly emerged from her dream and opened her eyes, Arnold's were right there to meet them.

When their eyes met, Mom knew she'd made it through, alive

and well, even as sedated as she still was. She was wheeled into recovery, where she relaxed for a while, but as evening came and the
anesthesia wore off, her wound began to hurt terribly.

She was still extremely weak and pale when the doctor came by
to see her the next morning.

"I'm happy to say that your surgery was a success, Mrs. Nussbaumer. Your pain will gradually subside," he said. "And you really will
feel better with each passing day."

"I hope so," Mom said, barely able to speak clearly. "I'm still in
terrible pain."

"Don't worry. The pain will pass," the doctor promised.

He continued to visit Mom every morning and was dismayed to
learn that her condition wasn't improving. The pain was so extreme
she could barely stand. She was also steadily losing weight and shed-
ding hair. It was all over her pillow—and she definitely wasn't yanking
it out herself. Finding all of this alarming, the doctors performed a
battery of tests.

The results they found were more alarming still, and they were
in no rush to share the news. Even though the bile duct had been
reconstructed, the first botched surgery caused bile to continue to
leak into Mom's abdomen, liver, and pancreas. This was the reason for
so much weight loss and pain.

When Arnold arrived one day with a friend in tow for support,
the doctor finally outlined the situation. "Your wife is seriously ill,
Mr. Nussbaumer."

He explained that the bile had leaked into her abdomen, liver,
and pancreas. It had frozen in her abdomen and couldn't pass through
the duct. Another invasive procedure was absolutely necessary, but
they feared she might be too weak to withstand it. "We know that she
won't be able to handle general anesthesia, but this is our last chance
to rectify the situation, so local anesthesia is the way we'll have to go."

Arnold felt as though he was about to collapse—and he looked
like it too. His friend grabbed a chair from the hallway and eased

Arnold into it. As if the doctor had been waiting all along for Arnold to be seated, he finally got to the bottom line: "I believe you're aware that the circumstances are life-threatening, Mr. Nussbaumer. But we'll do everything we can to save your wife's life."

"Don't tell her how serious it is," Arnold said quietly. "She's so weak right now, I'm not sure she can take it."

When my mother first met Arnold, he'd pleaded with her, "Please don't ever lie to me, Nexhi. Even if you've made a mistake that will hurt me like a knife in my chest, please remember that I'll always prefer to know the truth."

Obviously, that ethos perfectly matched my mother's. This shared dedication to truth has always been the glue of their marriage. It must have been excruciating for Arnold to instruct the doctors in this lie by omission.

Meanwhile, my mother lay in her bed, holding a cross. She wasn't religious, but she was attached to the cross because it was a gift I'd given her years before. It seemed to be her last hope, and sadly, it was all she had of me in that crucial moment. I was far away, busy courting my future in New York City, and I had no idea whatsoever that any of this was going on.

When Mom was about to be wheeled in for her third surgery, she requested permission to carry the cross with her into the operating room. The doctors quickly agreed; they had no time to waste. As they began rolling my mother's bed into the corridor, Arnold looked up balefully, as if searching for help in the ceiling tiles.

When he heard footsteps running toward him, he turned to find Blerti, who'd just arrived from Greece to be with his mother. The two greeted one another warmly and were grateful for each other's company as they sat together and waited for news.

XXX

I Kiss It and All
My Problems Go Away

THAT PARTICULAR TRIP TO NEW YORK STARTED OUT THE SAME AS ALL THE OTHERS. Once again, I felt at home the minute I stepped out of the terminal and onto the pavement at JFK. Everyone thought it was crazy to set my heart on the idea of becoming a model, but I had Mom as inspiration, and no matter the obstacles, she could do anything.

I was well aware of the setbacks she'd faced—when she was raising me back in Albania and in Switzerland when she took on the German language and turned a mere vision into a career.

When the going got tough, I knew that my mother took a breath—a moment to collect herself—and then she forged on. I'd watched her do it a thousand times. She was the original Powerfrau, and I was her only daughter; at least some of her competence and determination must have rubbed off on me.

Though it was well past New Year's, I remained completely oblivious to my mother's condition. It was never a surprise that she'd chosen not to tell me. She knew I was far away and that I'd worry—and what was the point in that?

But once upon a time, in New York, I had a horrible dream. My mother was crying, and I was kissing her belly. She wailed and cried, but there was nothing I could do but kiss her belly.

In the middle of the night, I got out of bed drenched in sweat. I grabbed my cell phone and dialed Mom's number.

No answer. I dialed again.

No answer. I dialed again.

Something's wrong. I just knew it. Then all of a sudden, my message tone signaled. There was a text from Mom: *I'm fine. Don't worry. I'll call you tomorrow morning.*

With trembling hands, I texted back: *Who is writing to me?*

I knew my mother hadn't sent that text. She never wrote to me without dropping in her affectionate nicknames and phrases. *Who is writing to me from my mother's phone?*

Almost instantly, my phone rang. It was Blerti. "Mom's in the hospital," he said. "She had to have gallstones removed, but she's fine now. She's just recovering from surgery. You don't need to worry."

I immediately burst into tears that continued to flow throughout the night. *Why wasn't I there? I should have been at her side!* There I was, celebrating the holidays, running around Manhattan, taking in all the bright lights and festivities, while my mother was in the hospital thousands of miles away.

I tortured myself all night, but the next morning, Mom called and tried to put me at ease.

"I'm fine, my love," she said, but her voice sounded weak and strained.

"Nothing is fine. I know it," I said through my tears.

"No, darling. I'm really fine now. I went through hell earlier, but the worst is over now."

She could hear me sniffling and crying through the phone. She must've felt as helpless as I did, as far from each other as we were. "I've been keeping your little cross with me all the time, my love. I kiss it," she said, "and all my problems go away."

Once again, she was far from me and there was nothing I could do. When I was ten years old, I worried all the time that she was hurt or sick or in distress. Now I knew for sure that she was suffering but—same as it had always been—there was nothing I could do.

XXXI

Peaks and Valleys

MOM SPENT AN ENTIRE MONTH IN THE HOSPITAL. It seemed absolutely endless, but she passed the time with visits from her students, who flocked to her bedside every day, bringing gifts and words of encouragement. The doctors were astounded to see so many women coming in and out of the hospital—far from a usual occurrence.

One doctor finally asked Arnold about my mother's steady stream of female devotees.

Arnold nearly glowed with pride as he explained. "These women are all Nexhi's students—participants in a project aimed at integrating Albanian, Kosovar, and Albanian Macedonian women into Swiss society. They admire Nexhi, and they love her as a teacher and as a human being."

"I appreciate Nexhi's commitment to her work," the doctor said, "but your wife really needs complete rest, Herr Nussbaumer. Why don't you cut off her mobile phone for a while and limit visits to family members for at least a few days?"

The doctor was right. Mom was extremely weak and still quite thin. It was crucial that she regain her strength. She still had a tremendous amount of progress to make in her recovery.

One day, as she lay in her bed, Mom suddenly felt terrible and called out to a nurse: "Please bring me some water. Nurse, please help! I'm not feeling well at all!"

The nurse ran to fetch a cup of water, but by the time she returned, my mother's pain had subsided. As quickly as the pain came on, it disappeared. These episodes recurred time and time again. She tried to remain stoic, but when the pain resurfaced, it was unbearable.

Throughout her four-week hospital stay, Mom endured an enormous amount of discomfort and was grateful whenever her physical distress would subside and she could just breathe easy for a little while. By all appearances, small amounts of bile were collecting in the drainage bag. She could only be discharged from the hospital when the drained fluids cleared and she seemed to be cleansing properly.

Once that occurred, the staff suggested that my mother stay at a rehabilitation clinic in the mountains, where she would be monitored and well cared for. The fresh mountain air also promised renewed health and vigor.

My mother mentioned her concerns to Arnold when he visited one afternoon. "I don't feel as though I can leave the hospital yet, dear," she said, "since I don't believe that I've fully recovered."

"No, my love, you're not going to a clinic," Arnold said. "We're going to St. Moritz, instead. Everything is arranged. Francoise and Otto are coming along. You know how much fun they are. I've reserved the best hotel rooms, with enormous windows and a great view of the roads and mountains. What do you think?"

It was February—just about the time of year when Arnold loved to go skiing—and my mother felt as much excitement as he did. With a loving glance toward Arnold, she agreed. He was so caring and so charming that if he said the sky was green, she'd probably consider the possibility. "Of course I'll go to St. Moritz," Mom said.

"I'd much prefer to be with you and our friends instead of going to a rehabilitation clinic alone."

Mom's doctor gave the plan his approval. "It will be most helpful—almost curative—for Nexhi to be with loved ones during her recovery."

A couple of days later, Mom checked out of the hospital and returned home for two days, where she relaxed and was grateful to be in her own bed. Once she'd rested up, my mother, Arnold, Francoise, and Otto left for St. Moritz. As a gift, Francoise presented Mom with a fur coat she'd inherited from her aunt, so that the recovering patient wouldn't be susceptible to the cold mountain air.

The couples had a beautiful time together, with Arnold almost always at Mom's side, catering to her every wish. When the gentlemen went skiing, my mother and Francoise took in the cold, crisp air from the hotel's terrace, in spite of the chilly winter wind.

Two weeks later, the four returned to Zürich. My mother felt refreshed and well, but she still hadn't regained her former strength and weight.

When I returned from New York, I went to visit, and I noticed that Mom wasn't herself. The moment I saw her, I burst into tears. She was thin and gaunt and could barely speak; she wasn't even steady on her feet. She tried to smile, pretending that everything was all right—a practice that she maintains to this day, even when things are less than perfect.

"Why are you crying, my Angela?" she asked.

"How can you ask such a question, Mom? I love you, and I know you better than I know myself, and you aren't at all yourself. You're not you! You're so skinny, and you can barely stand up." I hugged her and sobbed into her chest, soaking her dress. I needed her, and I certainly wasn't ready to see her like this.

"Look at me, Angela," she said, taking my face in her hands. "I am here, and I'm fine. I just need some more rest. Even the doctor told me that I look much better. I came through those three surgeries and that horrible ordeal in the hospital because of you. I said to myself, 'Angela needs me. I must be strong and get through this—for her.'"

If the doctor thought Mom looked *better*, I could only wonder what she looked like before. This was unacceptable. How could the doctors botch her surgery, send her to the mountains, and expect her to recover in the cold mountain air? What were they thinking? She was a shadow of herself, and I was unable to control my shock and despair.

Mom, on the other hand, declared that she wanted to return to work.

"No way," her doctor insisted. "You're not at all ready to return to your routine."

"But I must get back to work," Mom said.

"Mrs. Nussbaumer, you're a teacher, am I correct?" the doctor asked, regarding her with a look of disbelief and wonderment. "And how many classes do you teach per day?"

"I have six classes per day," she said. "But it's possible to reduce my workload to three or four classes if I take turns with one of my colleagues. You must understand, Doctor, I can't live without my job."

The doctor sighed but conceded. When a patient has been through so much, he explained, he liked to encourage their tenacity.

Mom looked at him with sincere gratitude. "Thank you, Doctor. This means so much to me."

Once she returned home, my mother confessed to Arnold her fear that the women of The Light might have lost interest in the project during her two-month absence.

Arnold smiled. "You must know by now that the women adore you. They can't do without you! Besides, the project has already been in effect for two years; you should have more confidence in it. Just wait and see the reception you'll get from your students when you return."

When Mom returned to work the following week, everyone greeted her with incredible warmth and love, just as Arnold had predicted. The women doted on her throughout each class, making sure she sat down during the lesson, instead of standing, as she usually did, in front of the students as they wrote in their exercise notebooks. As she tried to walk around to observe each student, someone was always there with a chair for her. "Please, Frau Nexhi, don't exert yourself," one women said, taking gentle hold of Mom's shoulders and guiding her into her seat.

At the end of each class, Arnold made sure that one of Mom's colleagues drove her home. "It's too soon for you to be traveling around the city alone," he said.

With so much attention wherever she went, Mom felt as though she were perpetually wrapped in a blanket of love and protection, and the healing process seemed to accelerate. When she went for a checkup a month later, the doctor was amazed.

"Have you already returned to work, Mrs. Nussbaumer?" he asked, surprised at her progress.

"I have, Doctor, and I'm thoroughly enjoying it," she said joyfully. "I feel much better now."

"I believe you've taught me a lesson," the doctor said. "When patients are allowed to do what they love most, they can, indeed, recover much faster."

Somehow, Mom always managed to offer meaningful lessons to the people around her—in the classroom and beyond it. She has always been inspired by the realization that she has inspired others. It's such a beautiful cycle. Think about it: as we inspire others, we each grow more inspired, pushing one another to ever greater heights of achievement and ever evolving aspirations.

XXXII

The Starting Line

EVERYBODY WAS SURE THAT THE MOMENT I TURNED EIGHTEEN, I'D BE OUT OF BASEL AND ON MY WAY.

Everybody was right.

I turned eighteen in May; I moved to Zürich in June. In the beginning, I moved in with my mom and Arnold. My mother was perfectly aware of my plans for my future, but still, she wanted me to go to school. We'd been over this a thousand times, and even though I knew my mother only meant well, I couldn't bear to go over it again.

Since I was nine years old and sent off to live with my father, I'd done what was best for everyone else.

I never complained to my father about Rita because I didn't want to cause any trouble between her and my dad.

I never complained to my mother about living with Dad and Rita because I didn't want my mother and father to start fighting.

I never fought to live with my mother because I didn't want my father to lash out—at himself or at anybody else.

I never admitted to my mother just how much I missed her, or just how terrified I'd been, or just how much hair I'd yanked from my own head wondering and worrying if I'd ever see her again.

I'd held back from saying any of that for years. Now the only thing I was willing to say was this: "I'm not going to school. I'm going to be a model, and I'm going to live in New York."

"For the past decade, *everything* I've done has been for somebody else. I'm done," I told my mother. "I'm only doing Angela from now on."

After that, we never had to go through the school discussion again.

"You deserve to live your dream," she said, and both of us sat together and cried.

By that time, I'd indisputably become a young woman. My distinct features along with my height and slim stature garnered me a fair amount of attention, but I had absolutely no idea how my modeling career might be launched.

...

One week later, in July, I went to Albania with Arnold and my mother for a family gathering.

We'd just landed at Nënë Tereza Airport—we hadn't even made it through customs yet—when, all of a sudden, I was officially a model.

Okay, it wasn't quite *official*, but there I was, waiting in the line at customs, and suddenly my dreams began coming true.

A customs officer approached me. "I must speak to you," he said. "Where are you from?"

"From Shkodër," I replied. "But I live in Switzerland now."

He asked how long I'd been away from Albania. "Since December 1996," I said. "When I was nine years old."

"Wait here," he instructed me as he dialed a number on his cell phone. He stared at me intently all the while. "Don't you go anywhere."

I wasn't entirely comfortable with this impromptu interrogation.

The reason I'd left Albania in the first place was to escape harassing and dangerous men.

The customs official spoke briefly on his phone, and then he handed it to me. The person on the line was Vera Grabocka, a key figure in the Miss Albania organization.

She told me that when I returned from my two-week family vacation on the beach, I should give her a call and we would arrange a meeting. I still don't know if this was destiny or just a fluke of good luck. All I know is that I hadn't stepped a foot on Albanian soil since I'd left nearly a decade earlier, and there I was back in Albania and all my dreams seemed to suddenly be coming true.

There's not a person in Albania who hasn't heard this story: Once upon a time, a young Albanian woman returned to her country after many years away. She'd barely made it off the plane before she was spotted. The next Miss Albania had just returned home.

If there's a moral to the story, I suppose it must be that sometimes a step backward is just the thing to set us on our way.

Once I returned from vacation, I had a meeting with the Miss Albania organization's Vera Grabocka. She encouraged me to become involved in the pageant, but nothing could persuade me to deviate from my plans.

"Thank you for your input," I said, "but my goal is to become a model in New York."

Recognizing my determination, Vera gave me the name of Fadil Berisha, a globally acclaimed Albanian photographer now living in New York.

...

Back in Switzerland, I lived with Mom and Arnold in Zürich for six months. I was grateful to bear witness to my mother's improving health. Her focus on the work she loved gave her motivation and strength; The Light was clearly a major factor in her continued healing process.

I held my first job as a bartender, and met my first boyfriend, James, at the gym, where he worked selling memberships. He'd managed to snag my number from the gym's database, and he called me. He was ten years my senior, and we moved in together. Throughout high school, my father had never even let me date. James fell in love with me, he said, because I had dreams. My ambition inspired him. We decided that both of us were really going somewhere, and we decided we'd get there together.

This was our plan.

In December 2004, just four months after the customs officer at Nënë Tereza Airport had jumpstarted my career, I called Fadil Berisha, the Albanian photographer whose number had been given to me, and I bought a ticket to New York to meet him and figure out how to take the next steps.

Fadil had immigrated to New York from Kosovo when he was nine years old. This youthful displacement was something we had in common. He was extremely supportive and encouraged me to enter the Miss Albania pageant. "Starting off here is very difficult," he said. "It's better to establish connections in Europe before trying to launch in New York."

"Pageants aren't my interest," I told him. "I'm going to move to New York and sign with Elite." Yet again, I couldn't be persuaded to recalibrate my dream. Or maybe I'd just had so long to picture my future that the image had become fixed. There was no changing it.

I had a session with Fadil, and I couldn't have been more excited about my new portfolio, which was now filled with his masterfully captured shots. It's impossible to explain the enormity of this step. It was no small thing to have his photos in your book, especially for someone just starting out. I was thinking about staying in New York to make the most of my momentum and my new connections. Fadil was having a holiday party at his studio, and, without any alcohol, I was completely buzzed. This was the world I'd conjured in my mind for so long, and there I was, right in the center of it. I wouldn't have been surprised in that moment if Mel B or Craig David had walked in the door.

Instead, that was when James walked in. He'd flown in from Zürich to pay me a surprise visit. It was the most romantic and courageous thing; I absolutely loved it.

"Come back to Zürich with me," he said. "Then we'll both move here together as soon as we're ready."

I was absolutely in love with him. *Oh, dear James. My first love!* My passion for him was enormous, and I was swayed by his charm and his devotion. He wasn't yet ready to move to New York, so it seemed best to make the move later, together.

I returned with him to Europe for Christmas, all the while thinking of my newfound and invaluable connection with Fadil. Fueled only by my dreams, my life had just started zipping off at an exhilarating pace.

Mom's heart swelled with pride, while Dad struggled with my modeling aspirations. James and I talked about moving to New York together. We'd do it one of these days, just as soon as he was as ready as I was to pursue his dreams.

I was eighteen years old and completely in love.

Then I was nineteen, then twenty, and I was going nowhere.

One minute, I'd been sitting with Fadil in his photo studio, and the next, there I was, back in Zürich. Two years had passed, and I was so depressed I could hardly scrape myself off the couch.

What would the original Powerfrau do in this situation? I wondered. I knew that my mother would take a breath, she'd collect herself, and then she'd forge onward.

I took a breath, I collected myself, and then I turned on MTV.

XXXIII

Starting Over

ONE DAY, MY MOTHER RECEIVED A CALL FROM ZÜRICH CITY HALL. She was asked to supervise integration language classes that were held in fourteen different languages. The program was called In Zürich Leben (Living in Zürich), and its goals were similar to those of The Light.

"Thank you for the offer," Mom said, "but I simply can't take it."

My mother had never turned down a teaching position in her life. "I'm tired," she explained. "I have a lot on my plate, and the truth is that I'm still weak after a series of surgeries."

The director, Rozana, was a lovely Italian woman married to a Swiss gentleman. "Please, Frau Nussbaumer," she begged, "we need a quality teacher, and I'm well aware that you're the best there is. What about teaching with us just once a week?"

Rozana persisted until Mother finally gave in.

Suffice it to say, Arnold wasn't pleased to learn that Mom had taken on yet another project. "Are you crazy, woman? Why are you doing this when you're still weak?"

"You know me, Arnold. You know I just love teaching, and I can't help myself."

The new project proved to be extremely fruitful and productive, the cultural content even more intricate than The Light's. In a discussion on the subject of health insurance, Mom explained that, as immigrants, the women unknowingly received less health insurance than Swiss citizens. She also explained the difference between legal and illegal jobs. My mother always found great satisfaction in sharing hard-won knowledge with women new to the country. It bolstered their self-esteem and emboldened them to take on the challenges their lives in Switzerland presented.

In each and every one of her classes, my mother took the time to speak to her students about truth. "You must make it a priority to speak the truth at all times," she said. This had always been her credo, and I was her first student of Truth, all those years ago when I mischievously stole her diamond ring.

While teaching In Zürich Leben, my mother's popularity snowballed—as did the number of students enrolled in her classes. At the beginning of the next academic year, thirteen teachers involved in the program gathered to introduce the students to the annual curriculum. Their meeting place was Karl der Große Zentrum, a Swiss center that offered integration and language courses for women.

A feminist activist, Suzana, worked tirelessly to protect women from spousal abuse due to alcoholism. Some of the women had faced this issue in their personal lives, so my mother frequently mentioned Suzana's name as a reminder to stand up for their rights and reclaim their freedom.

"You're very fortunate, ladies. Here you are, receiving vital information in your own language so that you can benefit from these courses to the fullest extent. When I first came to this country, I had a difficult time integrating, due to the language barrier. All of my classes were in German, which was completely foreign to me at the time," Mom explained.

The students always seemed to find inspiration in my mother. They were inspired by her courage and her facility with the language, and they aspired to her level of comfort in Swiss society. Recognizing the powerful impact of the program, Mom promoted her classes through her favorite method: word of mouth. And, once again, her success was astonishing.

Mom finally felt as though she'd arrived on stable ground—both personally and professionally. And medically, as well. Day by day, she became stronger and she slowly gained back some weight.

She and Arnold were supremely happy together, and they decided to build a little home outside the urban, hustle-bustle life of Zürich. Their place was in a little village on the outskirts of the city—a decision my mother later regretted, given the twelve-hour workdays that made the outskirts of the city feel much farther away.

Although money was never her motivation, she was pleased that her financial resources were growing. As a result, she was able to support her family in Albania. Despite spending so much time focused on integration, my mother had never lost sight of the importance of her home, her roots, and the people she loved.

XXXIV

Forging Ahead, MTV-Style

LYING ON THE COUCH AND WATCHING TV MIGHT NOT SEEM LIKE
A PARTICULARLY EFFECTIVE METHOD OF FORGING AHEAD—IT
DEFINITELY WASN'T A METHOD MY MOTHER WOULD HAVE USED—
BUT ONE DAY I TURNED ON MTV AND, ALL OF A SUDDEN, I WAS
INSPIRED AGAIN.

It had been more than two years since James and I returned to
Zürich from New York, and precisely nothing had happened with
my modeling career in all that time. I had Fadil's photos in my book
and some contacts in New York, but I was back to being a bartender,
and James was still working at the gym. We were supposed to be
moving to New York together, but it seemed impossible to muster the
motivation to get out the door.

At first I was waiting for us to come up with a plan together,
but James had no burning desires to motivate him—which, I later
realized, was the reason he said he loved me for my goals. He didn't
have any. If I was waiting for him to move to New York, it was
becoming clearer by the day that I'd be waiting a long time.

Depression and inertia had me stalled for months—or was it years? Either way, it was long enough that I'd stopped feeling stalled and I'd started feeling stuck.

But then I had the good fortune of catching a show on MTV about models in Miami.

I'd never really thought about the models in Miami. I'd been thinking about New York for so long, the other cities on the map had long ago disappeared.

I remembered that Fadil had told me it was better to build my book *before* landing in New York City. I knew I didn't want to build my book exclusively in the Albanian pageant world, but I had no problem with the idea of starting out my career by modeling in Miami.

The idea struck me like a lightning bolt, a hair-raising epiphany. I'd go build my book in Miami and *then* I'd move to NYC.

Duh! Why hadn't I thought of this before?

By the time James came home from work that evening, I'd already booked my flight. I told him that I'd bought a one-way ticket and I was leaving on Sunday.

As I packed, I kept reminding myself to bring my most important things even if I didn't think I'd need them. I already knew I'd never be coming back.

I thought of my mother and all that she'd been through with her two abusive marriages. I thought about how she'd courageously arrived in Switzerland alone, as lost as the women she'd made a career out of teaching. My mother learned the language; she learned the culture; she figured out her path through it and found recognition at every level along the way. Nothing could stop her. Nothing could stop me either.

Six days later, I was in the air and Miami-bound.

I'd booked a hotel for just one night with the following plan in mind: I had a list of modeling agencies, and first thing in the morning, I'd start visiting them one by one. I'd keep going for as long as it took for me to land a job and a spot in a models' apartment.

"What will you do if that doesn't work out?" James asked that night on the phone.

"It's going to work," I said.

"I think you should have a Plan B," he said.

"I don't want a Plan B." I really didn't. I was of the belief that if you didn't have a Plan B, Plan A simply had to work.

Having a Plan B spelled doom. It was a scaredy-cat move. If you had a Plan B, you probably didn't really believe you'd succeed at Plan A, and this latent self-doubt was bound to screw up your pursuit of it. Having a Plan B in place meant that you didn't really care if Plan A came through.

"Good luck," James said.

"Thank you."

In the morning, I checked out of my room and left my bag at the front desk. I had my list of agencies and I set out—walking. The list was organized by each agency's distance from the hotel.

I walked into the first agency, an open, airy space. I stood in the middle of it and announced myself. "Hello. My name is Angela Martini, and I have just come to Miami from Albania," I said. "I'm here to be a model, and this is my book."

Everyone was shocked and delighted. They laughed.

I laugh now just thinking about it. Can you imagine how thick my accent must have been back then? I was fresh off the plane, and I barely spoke English.

I presented the Polaroid pictures I'd brought with me. Sadly, the photos Fadil had taken of me three years earlier were now too old to show. I knew that Polaroids weren't the preferred format, but they were all I'd had on hand in Zürich, and once I'd made up my mind to get on that plane, I wasn't going to start scrambling around in a last-minute effort to buff up my book.

Having spent three years of my life in suspension, I wasn't going to wait a minute longer to get my show on the road. I was twenty-one years old—very late to be starting out as a model—and I wasn't going to let my broken English or my Polaroids stop me.

"We like you," said one of the women gathered around the table to look at my pictures.

The agency liked me! They looked at my book, took some pictures of me, and said they'd bring me on.

I knew it would work out. My heart thumped and I felt a lightness I hadn't felt in years. I was about to ask about getting set up in a models' apartment when the senior agent looked at me. "You have a working visa, right?" she said.

I had no such thing. They explained that they'd apply for the visa on my behalf—but I had to go back to Switzerland for six months and wait for it to be approved.

This was unimaginable. Absolutely not an option. The last time I went back to Zürich after a US career expedition, I'd ended up watching TV on the couch for three years. I stood on the street crying and called James.

"So come back for six months," he said. "What's the big deal?"

All of it, I didn't say. *All of it's a big deal.*

But as soon as I got off the phone, I had another epiphany. I ran back into the agency and said, "Hold on! I have a proposal for you."

I had figured it out. I'd work, build my book, and they didn't have to pay me until my visa came through. They could put the money in an account and deduct monthly amounts for providing me with housing and food. When I got my visa, the account would be mine.

"You're smart," said the senior agent.

They went for it. We'd worked out a deal.

I called James and my mom, and then I walked back to the hotel to pick up my bag, which I rolled over to the agency so I could take it to the models' apartment the agency had already arranged for me.

XXXV

Who's Here to Learn?

TENACITY ALSO RUNS IN OUR FAMILY, ANOTHER TATTOO ON OUR HEREDITY. As I focused on my next steps, Mom began her Albanian integration class at Karl der Große Zentrum.

The women adored her and instinctively understood that she wasn't in the teaching profession for money. Rather, she was driven by her passion, by her love for the work and the people she served. It was clear to her students that my mother's beliefs ran deep and she held fast to her ideas. Recognizing Mom's commitment to each and every one of them, students often became too devoted to her in return, class after class after class.

One of her male colleagues teased her during a lunch break, "Frau Nussbaumer, can you reveal your secret? Albanian women follow you everywhere you go."

Mom smiled. She knew it was a joke, but she'd grown tired of jokes with a lascivious subtext. Sometimes she got protective of her students, like a mother hen. When her women showed up for class they were making a deliberate effort to help themselves, and there was something undermining to that effort when they were seen as *women* rather than as *students*. Mom knew her colleague had been joking, but she also knew there was a larger cultural problem.

"You may find this strange, but I would venture to say that sometimes Communist methods work better. I was born and raised under the Communist regime."

A group of teachers laughed as she spoke.

"Tell us about the Communist methodology," the colleague said.

"The approach focuses, above all, on discipline, structure, and tending to each student individually," Mother explained in a serious tone.

"I couldn't agree with you more. That's what makes a true teacher," one of Mom's Swiss female colleagues affirmed.

"And the fact that the students are adults doesn't mean that they can do whatever they want in our classes," Mom said, turning her attention back to the man who'd initially started the conversation. "We must always remember that the women are here to learn. *Everybody* is here to learn, and that's the most important consideration."

XXXVI

How to Remember Your Dreams

THINGS TOOK OFF QUICKLY. I was booking steady jobs, and even when I hit a dry patch, my mother sent me funds directly from her own salary. It was a selfless display of love and generosity on my mother's part—sending as much as ten thousand Swiss francs a month while I was awaiting payments for jobs. These offerings weren't meant to be gestures of indulgence. Instead, she was bestowing on me a far more meaningful gift: my independence and the freedom to pursue my dreams without relying on a man.

Four months after I landed in Miami, I went to New York and signed with Elite Modeling Management—just as I'd always wanted. The only hitch was that I still didn't have a working visa, but Elite agreed to the same arrangement I'd suggested in Miami. I got a job working under the table at a steakhouse on the Upper East Side—even though my first job through Elite paid fifteen thousand dollars per day.

The money was grand, though I wouldn't actually see it until I got my work visa. But beyond money, they also sent me to New Orleans—which I loved. This was my first big shoot, and it was for Lily of France.

Fadil Berisha welcomed me to New York with open arms. Thanks to his guiding hand and kind heart, I was able to quickly adapt to life in the city. I found an apartment, and once I had settled in and was consistently earning substantial money, James's once-a-month visits became less and less significant to me. I wanted to be around fearless individuals who had dreams and goals like me. I was no longer at peace with the idea that, without my dreams to motivate him, James didn't seem to have dreams of his own.

Contrary to my mother's advice, I invited James to move in with me anyway. This was a mistake, but once again, my mother had set an example. This time it was an example of how to leave a man. When Mom and her first husband, Xhafer, split up, she left him with the apartment, deciding it wasn't worth the argument, she'd just find a new place on her own.

Once upon a time, in lower Manhattan, a young woman lived with a boyfriend she no longer quite loved. One day, when the boyfriend went out of town, the young woman found herself a new place to live. Not wanting to wait to be left or to spend precious time negotiating an agreement, the young woman left the boyfriend with the apartment they'd been sharing, and she found another place to rent on her own. She knew what she wanted, and so she paid three months of his rent in advance before moving on. That was the way the young woman had learned to leave a man.

...

In 2010, when I was twenty-four, Fadil finally convinced me to take his pageant advice. "Angela, listen to me. I want you to enter the Miss Albania and Miss Universe competitions. Consider it an act of pride in your ancestors and in Albania."

"It's too late," I protested. The Miss Albania competition began two weeks before the Miss Universe pageant in Las Vegas. There wouldn't be enough time for the standard one-year training period.

"Don't worry about all that," he said. "You'll learn as you go, and I'm here to help in any way I can."

First I flew to Albania from New York, entered the Miss Albania competition—and won! Then I flew back to New York to prepare for the Miss Universe pageant, which was taking place just two weeks later on the Las Vegas strip.

Fadil kept his word about helping me. He helped choose my costume—and he paid for it out of his own pocket. The dress was adorned with black and red wings, representing the colors of the Albanian flag. The flag's red color represents valor, while the double-headed eagle symbolizes Albania's sovereignty. The flag was first raised the year Albania achieved its independence.

Courage, independence, freedom. My country's motto really matters in my family. These words have always been the cornerstones of my mother's life and the cornerstones of mine. I wore my Miss Albania costume with great pride in my country, my family, and in my mother above all.

The experience of the pageant was unforgettable; I even shook the hand of future US president Donald J. Trump. The spectacle of Vegas somehow seeped into the pageant; to be in a pageant in Albania likely meant that you'd be hanging out in a gym. The Miss Universe event was a completely different animal. And walking through the casino in the hotel lobby was an experience in and of itself: all those miles and miles of headache-inducing carpets, the incessant clanging and chirping of slots and spilling of coins. And in the dressing room, all the other contestants—hopeful, cynical, ambivalent, determined, joyful, and longing—exactly like me.

I placed sixth among the eighty-three contestants from around the world. I had the pageant's highest ranking for any Albanian candidate in history. That record still stands. At home, my parents watched the event as it was broadcast on television, at four a.m. They cheered me on with zeal despite the early hour, and I swear that, in my heart, I heard every word of their love and praise.

Sometimes an experience is over before you have the presence of mind to enjoy it. The moment slips by while you're distracted, and then you get home, and the wonderful thing you've just experienced is nothing more than a blur.

At the Miss Universe pageant, I reminded myself to breathe deeply, trying to be present in every moment and take in every detail. There I was, living my dream, and I wanted to make sure I didn't miss it.

XXXVII

Life's Rewards

FEW THINGS BRING MY MOTHER AS MUCH SATISFACTION AS SEEING HER STUDENTS SUCCEED. Whenever she bumps into them out and about in Zürich, moving through the city with ease, she swells with pride and affection—and the feeling is mutual. Mom can hardly walk to the store without running into someone who rushes up to say hello and flex her German skills in Mom's honor.

All of them make a point of thanking my mother profusely. They call her their guiding light and credit her for leading their way to a future far more promising than they'd have realized on their own.

In her personal life, Mom couldn't be more content, but as she grew older, the subject of her retirement began to come up with increasing frequency in her conversations with Arnold.

"What am I going to do, sit around the house all day?" she kept telling him. "That's not who I am. You know I'm Powerfrau, not Hausfrau."[23]

"I know, I know. But you've already given so much to others, and

---

[23] *Housewife*

now is your chance to be selfish, to give to yourself—and also to me," Arnold teased.

Few things bring me as much satisfaction as seeing my mother's great love.

XXXVIII

Extraordinary Individuals

ONE OF MY SCARIEST MOMENTS IN NEW YORK WAS WHEN MY SEC-
OND APPLICATION FOR A WORK VISA WAS DENIED. This was really a
problem. "Two strikes and you're out," said a French friend who'd been
forced to return to her country repeatedly before getting a work permit.

Maybe visa denial is another hereditary marker in our family. How
could this possibly be happening again?

The only way I was going to be able to get a work visa at this
point was through the O-1 visa—the visa reserved for "individuals with
extraordinary ability or achievement."

"You can't get an O-one visa," said Fadil. "If you'd won a Nobel
Prize? Yes. If you were Gandhi? Yes. If you were J. K. Rowling? Maybe.
Miss Albania? Not going to happen."

I understood the problem: I wasn't an internationally famous model. I wasn't a world-renowned athlete. I wasn't a brainiac likely to make
an impact on America's social or economic development. I wasn't the
Albanian equivalent of, say, Ruth Bader Ginsburg or Steve Jobs. Nor
was I the spouse, child, or assistant of such an extraordinary individual.

But the O-1 visa was, in small numbers, also granted to individuals who seemed to fall short of extraordinary—figures who were far less established and from countries with limited opportunities in the arts, sciences, sports, or business worlds. I'd read about a Danish actress and an Israeli pianist, both in their early twenties, who had received O-1 visas. It was my only chance at this point. It was the unturned stone.

The application required letters of endorsement and agency sponsorship. It was no small feat to gather the materials, but I did and I sent them in.

"How's it going with the VIP visa?" my friends would tease as I waited.

I didn't want to go back to Switzerland. I knew that for sure.

"What's your Plan B?" asked a friend.

I shrugged. "I don't really believe in Plan Bs," I said.

I didn't want to be afraid, but I was.

One day, I was running along Fifth Avenue on my way to audition for a job, and I passed a fortune-teller who'd set up her table just outside Central Park. She had the headscarf, the big hoop earrings, and her tarot cards stacked on a small folding table. We made eye contact and I smiled. "I want to read your cards," she said.

"I would," I said, "but I don't have time."

I really would've, too, if I hadn't been in such a hurry. I kept going past her.

"Miss! Miss!" she called out to me.

I turned back to face her, not wanting to be rude, though I still kept moving, backing up step by step toward Central Park South.

"You're going to get good news!" she said.

My face broke into an involuntary smile. There was no reason to believe her, but of all the things she could've chosen to say, that was exactly the one I wanted to hear.

Later that same day, I learned that I had got the visa *and* I had got the job I'd just auditioned for. All the money I'd made since arriving in Miami came to me from my agencies in one big chunk, and I landed in an apartment in a building with a doorman in lower Manhattan. The day I moved in, I thought about the conversation I'd had with my mother back in Switzerland. "I want to do Angela," I'd told her. "I'm going to do Angela now."

And just as Mom had done time after time after time, I'd taken a deep breath, I'd gathered myself, I'd forged ahead, and there I was: twirling my keys around my finger as I walked around the new apartment I'd be calling home as, at long last, I really got to be Angela.

...

Once upon a time, a baby girl was born in the middle of the road in an Albanian village.

Once upon a time that baby girl grew up to have a baby girl of her own.

They loved each other very much and lived together in Albania—until they were separated by social upheaval and civil war.

The mother sent her daughter to safety in another country. "I'll be there soon," the mother said. "I'll be right behind you."

But this reunion took far longer than either of them had imagined. They pined for each other. They worried about each other. They cried themselves to sleep.

The mother struggled in ways she can't bear to mention.

The daughter struggled in ways she can't bear to mention.

Still, both managed to forge ahead.

One day, the mother and the daughter along with two other people they loved, found themselves all together in New York City. It was the holiday season, and the city was decked out in garlands and bows, the shops and the streets and the trees done up in twinkling lights. The street-corner Santas rang their bells, and the sidewalks were crowded with people peering into the department store windows done up in holiday displays.

The mother, the daughter, and the two other people they loved were ready to take a break from the crowds, so they decided to take a horse-and-buggy ride around Central Park.

They sat close to one another in the small carriage seats, cozy under woolen blankets that kept out the chill. They were so far from the dusty road where the mother had been born and so far from the tiny bed in which the daughter had spent so many nights longing for her mother.

Here they were now, together, as the horse's hooves clomped along the park's paths. As they forged onward, the mother and daughter each took a deep breath; they were both living their dreams and wanted to be sure they realized it.

Epilogue

Lessons and Legacy

SOME PEOPLE STRUGGLE WITH THE QUESTION OF WHETHER OR NOT THEY SHOULD WRITE AND PUBLISH A BOOK. Not me.

I have a brilliant life story built into my family, and it's my duty and pleasure to tell it.

My mother's name is Nexhmije Ibrahimi Nussbaumer, and I am a living testament to her philosophies. Chief among them is her belief that nothing is finished until there is a happy ending—until you reach the light.

The light: it has been her goal, her business, her professional function, and her nickname for me.

For me, she is a radiant role model. Inspired by her, I've become an ardent feminist and an independent thinker; I've learned to trust my own instincts and maintain my determination to achieve my goals, even in the face of setbacks. All of this requires a sort of fearlessness. So if there's a single concept that underlies my personal mantra, it's Fearlessness.

Be fearless, I remind myself. *Stay fearless.*

Of course, none of us are truly fearless, but my mother's life experiences have shown me that I must not cower before the unknown. Being fearless means seizing opportunities wherever they exist.

Being fearless means never allowing people or circumstances to get in the way of your goals.

Being fearless means loving like you've never been hurt before.

Being fearless means forging a path through darkness to arrive at the light.